I0622181

THE MIND'S EYE SHATTERED!

Motivational Poetry, Songs & Short-Stories

Written & Published by

(New Edition)

D. Tobias Turner

48HRBOOKS.COM

48HRBOOKS.COM

Editors note: "THE MIND'S EYE" was first published in 2010"now the author brings you "THE MIND'S EYE SHATTERED!" with his first publication in 2020. Cover page was created by the author and formulated by the designers at 48hrbook.com. The back cover and dedication photos were provided by the author. Co-Editor: Jenay Lyles.

Printed in the United States of America

DEDICATION

TO MY SON: THE THINKER

TOBIAS DEOPOLIS TURNER

"Education cost, but ignorance cost more..."

ACKNOWLEDGEMENTS

ALL CREDIT BELONGS TO GOD FIRST. WITHOUT HIM TOUCHING MY MIND, THESE BOOKS WOULD HAVE NEVER BEEN WRITTEN.

ALSO, I WOULD LIKE TO THANK THE PEOPLE WHO INSPIRED SOME OF THE EXCERPTS, FROM EXPERIENCE, JOYFUL MOMENTS, AND GREAT LOST. FOR THE READERS OF MY 1ST BOOK-THANKS FOR THE ENCOURAGEMENT YOU'RE THE REASON FOR THE 2ND "THE MIND'S EYE SHATTERED!"

MY BOOK FOR ALL FOREIGNERS WHO WANT TO KNOW HOW THINGS IN AMERICA GO, THEN MY BOOK WILL LET YOU IN ON THE SHOW.

MY CHILDREN, FAMILY AND FRIENDS: ACROSS THE UNITED STATES, INCLUDING THOSE IN ASIA, EUROPE, NORTH AMERICA, AND THE CARRIBEAN. I LOVE YOU ALL BIGTIME! SPECIAL THANKS TO MY DAUGHTER AND CO-EDITOR: JENAY LYLES.

MUST READS!!!

POETRY SECTIONS: HAT'S OFF!...AN APPRECIATION OF LIFE!...A LOVE CASTLE...SELF-SERVING LIES!...WHITE DEATH!...LIVING LIFE IN A BOX!...FIGHTING YOURSELF!...JUST NEXT THEM!

STORY SECTIONS: SWEET AIR LANE...YOU AIN'T WHITE ENOUGH! (THE BIG-PAYBACK!). "Soul-Flow!" (SERIES).

"Soul-Flow!" IS AN EXCEPTIONAL HERO DEDICATED TO PROTECTING THE 'HOOD!' HE ONLY COMES OUT AT NIGHT. HIS UNTIRING EFFORTS TO HELP OTHERS IS UNMATCHED AND HE ALWAYS GETS THE JOB DONE.

SO, I INTRODUCE TO YOU THE NEW WAVE OF 'SUPER-HEROES' IN MY 'BAD-HAIR-DAYS!' & 'TALES FROM THE HIP!' COLLECTION...GOD BLESS!

INTRODUCTION

THIS COLLECTION OF MOTIVATIONAL POETRY, AND CONTEMPORARY WORKS, ARE INTENDED TO OPEN YOUR MIND AND HEART, TO THE WORLD OF IMAGINABLE THINKING. IN THIS REAL WORLD, WE ONLY WANT TO DIRECT YOU TO POSITIVE THOUGHT.WHERE LIFE CARRIES BOTH NEGATIVE AND POSITIVE. WE OFFER FOUNDATIONS TO BUILD SOLUTIONS, AND BRING OUT THE BEST IN ALL OF US, FOR A MORE UNIFIED WORLD.

WE OPEN WITH THE INFAMOUS 'HOUSE-HOLD READS' COLLECTION, FOR DAILY MOTIVATION AND AWARENESS; TO GIVE FOCUS ON THE REALITIES OF LIFE, AND BAND-WAGON YOU TO SUCCESS. IN HOPE, THAT WE KNOW SOMEONE WHO HAS BEEN PLEAGUED WITH LIFE-PROBLEMS, IN NEED OF A REALITY CHECK: OR NECESSARY TO BRING PEOPLE CLOSER TOGETHER; IN THE SPIRIT OF HARMONY. THE INFAMOUS 'HOUSE-HOLD READS' CAN STABILIZE YOUR COMMITMENTS TO POSITIVE CHANGE.

AS WE SHIFT GEERS, IN THE POERTY IN MOTION SECTION; WHICH COVERS SEVERAL DIFFERENT ASPECTS OF FOOD FOR THOUGHT; INTENDED TO MAKE YOU LAUGH, CRY, THINK, AND QUESTION THE UNANSWERED. THE IDEA IS TO LOOK AT LIFE WITH SERIOUS EYES, AND BE YOUR OWN HERO. SOME ARE SERIOUSLY DEDICATED TO OFFSETTING THE PAIN OF THOSE SUFFERING. OTHERS, A TRIBUTE TO VALIANT EFFORTS, BY THOSE WHO GO THE EXTRA MILE. ALL IN ALL, A WAKE UP CALL: FOR THOSE LOOKING FOR APPRECIATION AND GUIDANCE. THIS COLLECTION IS BONUSED WITH SELF-APPRAISING POETIC-JINGLES AND SONGS, FOLLOWED BY POETIC-STORIES OF VILLIANS AND HEROES. ALL INTENDED TO GIVE YOU A MENTAL-CLIMAX, ON THE ROLLER-COASTER RIDE OF LIFE.

FOR ANY AND ALL REQUEST, YOU MAY CONTACT THEAUTHOR AT:

TOBIAS.TURNER@HOTMAIL.COM

OR MAKE A PURCHASE OF "THE MIND'S EYE" COLLECTION, AT:

LULU.COM

48HRBOOKS.COM

INDEX

THE HOUSEHOLD READS COLLECTION
(Section I)

POETRY IN MOTION
(Section II)

INDEX
(CONTINUES)

BONUS SECTIONS:
1. **CHARACTER LISTINGS**
2. **THE LYRICAL MASTER (LIST OF SONGS-AVAILABLE)**
3. **COMMENTARY-SUMMARY**

SECTION I

THE HOUSEHOLD READS COLLECTION

THE MIND'S EYE DEFINED!

GATHER ROUND AS I RUN IT DOWN,

WHILE I UNRAVEL WHAT THIS BOOK WAS MEANT TO BE.

THE AUTHOR HAD HOPE, GOD GAVE HIM SOME ROPE,

TO HELP SET A STATE OF JUBILEE.

WONDERS NEVER CEASE, WHEN MINDS RELEASE,

GREAT THINGS WE ALL UNDERSTAND.

SOME BRANDED WITH STYLES, THAT LAST FOR AWHILE,

BUT DEFINITION WILL ALWAYS STAND.

WHERE POLITICIANS PROW, AND LAP-DOGS GROWL,

IN SEARCH OF THAT MUCH NEED FOR A SHOW.

WHERE BELIEVERS WIN, WITH A BIBLE FRIEND,

AND FOUND GOLD AT THE END OF THE RAINBOW.

THIS BOOK HOLDS TRUE, TO SOME THINGS BORROWED,

SOME THINGS VIEWED, AND SOME THINGS NEW.

LET TRUTH AND FANTASY RELEASE, TO BRING FORTH

PEACE, FOR GOOD DEEDS WE ALL CAN DO.

Hat's Off!

"Hat's Off!" to the women who are True and Divine,
Demonstrating a Kind Heart
and keeping the Family in line.
For Guiding your Sisters to be like you are,
With Wisdom and Character born from a Star.
Where there are no decent women
there are no decent men,
Thank you so much for your 'Magic Touch'
and being a constant friend.
For showing them that Marriage is life
and not a Game,
When you made "The Virgin Mary"
smile all over again.
That Love is not an Art it's Life Plus One,
For raising the 'Bar' higher under the Joyous Sun.
Words cannot express your sparkling attitude,
Without women like you
the Devil would continue to Rule.
So we take our 'Hat's Off!' to you
to show our Respect,
Because without women like you
there would be none left.
Respect is earned and courtesy is given,
Thank GOD for making someone like you
to make life worth living!

The Honey Cone Highway

Lakes rivers and streams laden
with fruit trees of every delight,
A land lovers' Dream of Romantic Islands in Paradise.
Passages of Vegas-Styled-Shows
and Amusement Parks for all to go.
Captivating colors of light brighten the night,
There's music and dancing under the Moonlight.
Bikini clad beach goers catching some rays,
A Smorgasbord of all you can eat
and desserts special made.
And the fun never stops with the 'Hit Parade'.
Spiral staircases leading down to a Piano Bar,
Or catch a glass elevator for a show with the Stars.
All Tux and Tails and Formal Dresses
for the Filet Mignon,
Seems like a Fairytale with the Magic Wand.
Champagne Glasses toasting to a Duty-Free-Spin,
As you pass a Casino where Underdogs Win.
Some petting and pampering or a message at the Spa,
Where everyone's made to feel like a Star!
People from all over the World for you to get to know,
Nothing But choices of party spots to go,
or just sit in on a Comedy Show.
Shop until you drop like the Malls
with Cascading Sounds,
It was just a Cruise Ship making the rounds.
Not a care in the World from everyone's laughter,
" The Honey Cone Highway "...is taking all Passengers!

All IN!

"All In"...To Free My Mind I Had To Let Love Go
And Give My Other Lover A Chance.
When It Starts Scratching At My Mind,
To Let "The Black Sword" Dance!
Like Fine Art on a Canvass,
"All In" Just Demands It.
Practice Makes Perfect To Sing That Song,
Whoever Wrote It, Did It On Their Own
Something In The Parts We Play,
You're Either "All In" Or You Miss That Stage.
The Thought That Weighs Less Than A Feather,
May Never Ever Come Back.
Like That Shadow We Carry Along,
Always The Color Of Black!
That Disappears When The Light Goes Out,
A Long-Standing Fact.
The 'Mind's Eye' Opens,
With Messages of Knowledge For You To Extract.
"All In", Even The Wind Speaks To Me
With That Special Sound A la mode,
Or Like Crashing Waves That Grabs The Mind,
For Some of "The Greatest Stories Ever Told".
Each Waking Moment These Thoughts
Keep Humming In my Mind,
Wakes Up The Hand That Drives 'The Black Sword',
To Bring Musical Thought, Line by Line.
Shaping my Challenge For Thinking,
With That Other Lover of Mine.
'All In' For Me Demands It,
Another Precious Gift from 'GOD', Oh So Divine.

So Please Excuse,
While I Frame The Power of 'All In',
That Needs To Be tapped!
My Other Lover Calls To Me,
Another Feather Under My Cap.

The World On Pause!

" I can't hear myself think!...
Shut up in there!" (Parenting).
" GOD'S " got 'The World On Pause' and said,
" Everybody Stop and Think.
Take a Closer Look at Life!
It can End with a Blink."
So in The Blink of an Eye we Cry,
When the Angel of Death comes we Stop,
And when we lose the One's we Love...we Think.
Sometimes it takes The Shadow of Death
 to get our Attention.
To appreciate the Now, to Canvas our Surround.
Like a child put in Time-Out
to think of the things he did,
What's Your Next Contribution going to be,
 if Given a 2nd Chance?
Well, " GOD " has 'The World On Pause',
to give You a Better Glance.
Take a Closer Look at Life!
" GOD's World"...and everything in it.

An Appreciation Of Life!

It may all sound tempting a Good-Fist-Fight,
But if it's not "Paid-Per-View"
you don't get 'Paid' tonight.
Women not speaking for years
because she had her shoes on,
Men once 'Bonded by Blood'
won't answer the phone.
Sisters out there 'Battling' over the same Man,
A Fool in the Group thinks he's a One-Man-Band.
Now 'Haters' are asking that 'You' not be a Fan,
When Bullets start flying where will they land?
We need to 'Squash These Beefs'
in this 'Motherland'.
The 'New World Order' who wants to run it All,
Atrocities of Life with Mass Graves
where Empires Fall.
A Suicide Bomber is ready to Attack,
This still won't bring his Family back..
A Mass Shooting signaled at another School,
Why Die so young when you don't have to.
So do me a favor and make a 'Sacrifice',
Squash these 'Beefs' and show
"An Appreciation Of Life!".
People with attitudes that just won't let it go,
Put Love in Your Heart turn up the Radio.

Stolen Sunday

Somebody 'Stole Sunday"... what?!
The Rest-Day of Peace and Quiet,
The Day of Meditation and Prayer,
The Day we Honored our Neighbors,
The Planning for Next-Week Sunday.
The Noise and Drama are supposed to be Resting.
Games of Chance, Romantic Sin
and Thievery still work on Sunday.

"Well how can we get our Sundays Back?"
'Just put back what was Missing.'
"So, have you ever done any of the above?"
'Yes, Imperfect me did All of Them.
We All have...even a Baby will 'Bite' you on Sunday.'

Read it and Weep!

Proud Out Loud!

Nervousness hampered and securities pampered,
We won't be bothered right now.
As you walked down the Aisle
with that Amazing Smile,
Oh, how you've made me so " Proud Out Loud! "
A Day to remember our Special Moment in Time,
Something so nice that feels just right,
we are the Fruit on the Vine.
With our Visions of Hope for a better life,
Taking your Hand and never letting go
of my Gifted Wife!.
On this day we'll share Our Dream
with Heart Felt Memories,
Where I'd take yours and give you mine,
for the Whole Wide World to See.
Passions Paraded with colors of Pink Roses
and smiles locked in a Maze,
Sealed with a Kiss on the Tastiest of Lips,
bound for Better Days.
Forever Blessed to be given a Gift like You,
And Forever Thankful...
 that The LORD Our GOD came through.
Amen to that, Amen to US,
HE is where we'll place Our Trust!

Amen!

In A Class By Yourself

When you keep doing things like nobody else,

You must realize 'You're In A Class By Yourself'.

Able to get it done in a calculating way,

Working all night and pushing all day.

Fine tuning the Arts in your own 'Special Way'.

Bringing New Styles, got the Crowd all Wilded!

Smoothing the rough and Calming the Heat.

Amazing and Blazing all 'Monu-feak',

Staying ahead of 'The Game' week, after week.

Some will never understand

the Stripes You've Earned.

They keep stealing Ideas

from the things you've Learned.

They want to 'Stop' your flow before you take off,

You're 'In A Class By Yourself'

where others get lost.

Stay Strong it's coming, your 'Just Reward',

Man can't give it, it's already yours.

A Love Castle

Warmth Flows Through Every Wall,
Filled with 'True-Hearts' and Unselfish Arms.
With Promises Kept and Dreams Fulfilled Inside.
A Kitchen Full Of Deliciousness of Mouth-Watering
Desserts, With Fruit-Top Ceilings.
A Family-Room Where Fun Never Ends.
A Bedroom Where Love Begins Continuously
And Passions Have Satisfaction.
Huggs and Cuddles Mixed With Tender-Kisses.
A Foundation Of Memories
With Thirst Quenching Flavors,
The Master of Arms Secures
and The Mother of Nature Ready.
Like Sun-Rays, Love Flows
Through Every Door and Window,
Bringing Forth Light Day and Night.
Seasoned With Support
for Encouragement and Motivation,
All Embedded and Willfully Given
To Produce Finishers and Winners!
Unsealed From Time So Life Can Breathe Freely.
Soulfully Rich Without Bondage
For A Natural Self-Confidence.
This 'Palace' Called 'Love Castle' is Home.
An Entanglement of Strong Intimate Thought
Built From Love.

Self-Serving Lies!

The Best tooth-paste and mouth-wash
can't brush away these Lies,
They floss to twist the truth and gargle as they Spy.
Looking for their next victims of 'Self-Serving-Lies!'
Little White-Lies didn't know they had color,
Black Friday can you show me how to find it,
my Calendar has no other.
In a time where trust got thrown out the window,
And assurances need some help.
Lies roll off their tongues
and they Brag amongst themselves.
A Man's Word was his Bond no more,
A Handshake to 'Seal the Deal' not sure.
They live all over the Internet and have no regrets.
You'll spend time uncovering the Truth
and cleaning up the Mess.
You want Guarantees, please put it in writing.
The Courts are full they're fighting like Vikings.
Broken Promises by your Best-Friend,
now you have no Respect.
Don't Bet your Pockets,
while Liars continue to swarm the Hornet's Nest.
They Murdered the Guilty Conscience a Long time ago,
With 'Self-Serving-Lies' and Straight-Forward Eyes,
I Wish I could soften the Blow.
So what you learned in the Past
about Honor, Dignity and Trust.
No one is spared in this New World of Lies and Secrets
No If's No Ands' or Butts'!

Not Use To Money

You ever see a person just lose their mind,
When they get Money it should've been a Crime.
While acting a Fool they can't see
that other kind of Thief,
That likes to hit a lick and come up Quick!
They All Target A 'Smiling Fool' that they call 'Trick!'
Having Million-Dollar-Parties while people still starving.
Buying stuff that you don't need
or Buying everything that you see.
When, really none of it fulfills their needs.
Can't even see why they're All coming around,
with Greedy-Grins and Friendly now.
Out there spending money 'All out of Control',
Or other People's Money in your hand, 'Fool's Gold.'
The Consequences of being 'Broke'
 never crossed your mind.
Or losing a Real-Friend, who trusted you one time!
A Fool with Money is the Worst,
when they're 'Broke' again then it Hurts!
Never took a moment to plan a move,
With the wrong people around, 'Eyeing A Fool!'
Got you 'Hating' on 'Real-Friends',
who were there for You!
Just 'Not Use To Money', what a waste,
'People' working hard, trying to catch a Break.
But they gave it to a 'Fool' who can't see straight!
Another Millionaire Gone-Broke,
A 'Chance of a Lifetime' up in Smoke!

White Death!

What's My Name?... COCAINE!
What's The Price?... You Spend All Night!
Who Does COKE?... Stupid Folks.
Some Call Me, "The All-Mighty-Girl!"
I'll Dance Through Your Mind And Rule Your World!
I Have Lots Of Names, Like "Snow" And "Blow!"
Take Your Pick, I Won't Say "NO!"
From Status Bearers To 'Ghetto-Looters',
From 'Tooters', To Lovers Of "Straight-Shooters!"
Like A Magician, It's Just An Illusion.
Like Me Too Much And Go Into Confusion.
Like Most Lovers Of Me, You Won't Quit!
No Matter The Cost, You'll Take The Hit.
I'll 'Over-Inflate' Your 'EGO',
Disrupt Your Nerves And Won't Let Go!
I Make Men & Women Ask For More,
Betray Your Best-Friend Who Lives Next Door.
I Turn Men Into Boys,
To Lose Their Dignity And Ask For More.
I Turn Women Into 'Freaks',
To Lose 'Self-Respect' Where No One Speaks!
I Fill-Up Grave-Yards,
Put You In Prison Or Watch You Starve!
Make You Sleep On The Street,
I'm With You Until You Land On Your Feet.
So, Why Don't You Try Me And See?
I'll Take You Around The World, But It Won't Be Free!
I Bear The "Skull And Cross-Bones" On The Left,
Be Another Victim Of Me,... "White Death!"
And If You Don't Ask Me For Help!
Then Try My Brother, "Boy-Heroin" ... "Black Death!"

SECTION II

POETRY IN MOTION

The Mind's Eye Shattered!

Mirroring Each Other In Progress,
Matching Zeal With That Cardiac Feel.
Weathering Storms Where Challenges Matter,
"The Mind's Eye" And "The Mind's Eye Shattered!"
A New Wave Of Mental Thought Crafted And True,
Sensationalism Captured Just Playing A Tune.
Creations From The Depths Of The Soul,
As life Opens Up Imaginations Unfolds.
A Series Of Memories And Epithets,
Bringing Forth New Characters, Wearing New Hats.
Effervescent Reflections Of Mental Light,
Brings *The Mind's Eye Shattered!*"
Beaming So Bright.
A Partner To Hold In The 'Heat Of The Night',
Or Daytime Twins,
Walking The Sands Where Life Has Friends.
For The Love Of "The Mind's Eye" Brings
'The Mind's Eye Shattered!"
The Twin-Towers Of Power
Where The 'Third Eye Matters'.
It Rains Down The Physical,
The Heart's An Open Book,
Venture Down " The Mind's Eye Highway "
...And Take A Second Look!.

Living Life In A Box

"GOD" threw him a ladder to climb out of the Box,
Then "GOD" cut doors for him to walk out of the Box,
 "GOD" even made a tunnel for him to leave the Box,

Like someone who couldn't fight his way out of a paper-bag,
He Died in that Box.

"For crying out loud! Where were you 'LORD?'
I needed you now I'm Dead."

GOD ANSWERED:

"Ladders are made for climbing and Doors could have been opened,
And a crawl to Freedom could have saved your Life."

Boxed in or Boxed out, when Life walls you in and you're Living In Doubt.

When you need answers revealed to your Mind,
"GOD" said... "Call ME."
"No cell phones please."

Digital Temper Tantrum!

Blowing up and can't Stop!
They made you 'MAD' and got you Hot!
Dropping 'Adult Bombs' with a Fuse,
The Digital World has it's 'Eyes' on you.
Sounds like a Terroristic Threat.
Airing your problems, All over the Internet.
Some might laugh other's might Shout!
Raising 'HELL' like All-Get-Out!
Undercover Agents got their eye on You,
The Watch-Dogs of Internet like finding the 'Fool".
End up in a cell or lose your Job,
Party-Crashers bringing down 'Hostility',
like the Mob.
There goes another Internet Freak in Cuffs.
Now your "Digital Temper Tantrum"
got you All Messed Up!
So just keep it 'Private'...
why throw yourself under the Bus.
Cyber-Trails have a path of it's own,
Confront People Direct...
and stay off of the 'Damn Phone!'

Fighting Yourself!

Fighting Yourself= When you won't try Something New!

Fighting Yourself= When you Don't take your Opponent Seriously!

Fighting Yourself= When you're Living A Lie!

Fighting Yourself= When You Let Drugs Rule!

Fighting Yourself= When you're Afraid To Do It From Scratch!

Fighting Yourself= When You Keep Carrying The Weight of Others!

Fighting Yourself= When You Refuse To See The Big Picture!

Fighting Yourself= When You Won't Think Outside The Box!

Fighting Yourself= When You Won't Take A Different Approach!

Fighting Yourself= When You're Your Own Worst Enemy!

Fighting Yourself= When You Keep Over-Thinking It!

Fighting Yourself= When You Refuse To Put In The Work!

Fighting Yourself= When You Let Others Control Your Moves!

Fighting Yourself= When You Don't Believe In You!

Fighting Yourself To Be Yourself...

Glazed Donuts!

Looking All Delicious! Keep that in Mind,
Dancing with Donuts happens All the Time.
This is not about 'Crispy's Cream' or 'Donkey's Donuts!'
It's about 'Thirst-Trappin'
with 'Sleek Bodies' and 'Brazilian Butts.'
Bodies and Booty's All Oiled and Sweaty,
Toned-Out for All To See,
Now Posing and Flexing on the Internet
showing That 'Eye-Candy!'
A Skimpy-Swim-Suited Body coming out of the Pool,
Groupies All Fashioned and Prancing Through,
Sweeter Than Cream and Making New Rules.
Just Showing Enough Skin is not Enough,
They're Reaching for The Flavor of 'Glazed-Donuts.'
If you ever want to know what 'Fame' Tastes Like,
Now Here They Come 'Thirst-Trappin'
All Day and All Night.
The Cameras are on and Eyes are Opened
To Captivate the Fans,
Anything to Lock Down Their Named-Brands.
The Prime of Delight Leaving a 'Tasty-Freeze' Trail,
Visual Sexy and 'Glazed- Donuts'
Flavorized to Boost Their Sales.
To All The Beach-Nuts and Weekend-Warriors,
This one's on The House,
'Thirst-Trappin' is What This Competition's All About.

Tugging At My Heart

He Won't let go of This Magic Show,
Pulling Like Puppets on A String.
It's more Than Smoke and Mirrors,
When it's A Wonderful Thing.
That background Sound and Theme Keeps Playing,
Like Weights on my 'Heart' Holding it down,
Walking Through my Mind
without Uttering A Sound.
Surrounded By His All Natural,
His Scents, His Smiles, those lovely Eyes.
With Curtains of Love Behind them.
My Mind, Body and Heart Just Explode!
The Most Beautiful Thing About Him,
He's 'Tugging At My Heart' and Won't let go.
That Seldom Found 'Heavenly' Match,
Rising To New Heights, by A Guiding Light.
A Masterpiece Unto Itself,
True Love Breathing from His Core,
'Tugging At My Heart'... I'm Addicted.
" Curtains Of Love"...

Help Don't Care!

Help Don't Care where it comes from,
If you don't Mind, It'll Be on Time.
Thanks To Those Who Give In The Blind.
Touched By 'GOD' and Friends of Mine.
Recognizing hard Times When The Cupboards Bare,
When It Looks Like It's Pass Time
by The Shoes you wear.
When Your Stomach's Rubbing your Back,
Good Smells brings Headaches That Leaves Tracks.
Some In The Grind, Others In A 'Food-Line,'
Thanks for The Gifts That was so Kind.
That Made The Day, In A Special Way.
'Help Don't Care' Where It comes from,
No Strings Attached You Had Our back.
Some Might Bypass But You Gave,
Just An All Out Thanks, with A Signature Wave.
To Share The Wealth Inside Yourself.
You Treated Others' Special Above All Else.
I Noticed You weren't Rich At All,
Just Open-Minded To The Call.
When The Genuine Stand Together,
It's Better Than A Love Letter.
When You Need It Now and "Proud Out Loud!"
'Help Don't Care Where It Comes From,
Not Just The Slums but The Working Ones.

Love's Prison

The Heart knows what it wants,
Ran Out of Gas Then It Fizzles.
Nothing Left In The Tank, The Pockets,
The Travel, The Waiting.
Get There Too Tired for Love Making.
Catch Your Breath It's Time To Go,
The 'Long-Goodbye's and 'Strong-Hello's.
Love Worn Down Like an Old Pair of Boots,
Blind To The Consequences of Love without Roots.
It Started with Skyscrapers and Trips To The Moon,
Love Needs Daily Nurturing In Order To Bloom.
Or Choke Like Weeds Where Flowers Use To Grow,
No Fault of Their Own When 'Cupid' Shot That Arrow.
Unbeknown To Them, That's Half The Battle,
Lonely Days and Lonely Nights
Unreal Suspicions Take Flight.
Argue To Make Up Starts To Consume,
What Was Once 'Real Love' With No Silver-Spoon.
A Seed Can't Grow In Two Places,
Try Holding A Deck of cards With Only Two Aces.
Try Ten thousand miles of Separation,
To Give you A 'Love Prison' of 'Distant Lovers',
as a Destination.
Try 'Kissing The Baby' in The Sunshine,
Time to Go, Time To Leave It Behind…"Now It's Dark".

The Long Handled Spoon

Dogs bite when animals fight,
And Lions Roar to go at it some more.
Like Wonders that never cease,
They push too far and cut too deep.
Like Wolves locked in a net,
All for the challenge with no respect.
This savagery works in the Wild,
But when it comes to people it's out of Style.
In order for some to Blossom and Bloom,
You must feed these Bullies
with a 'Long Handled Spoon'.
You can never quench their thirst,
The more you give, they only get worse.
For 'GOD' placed them under the Moon,
And fed them All with a 'Long Handled Spoon'.
For the Family that Preys has no Light,
Doomed for Harsh Labors and Sleepless Nights.

Public Love

Not behind closed doors with 'Private Huggs',
Passions of Affection with Gestures of Love.
Real Couples Love anytime any place,
Without Hidden Agendas trying to save face.
Sunset's a Blaze the Real Plateau,
Something Lovers Dreamed of A long Time Ago.
Counting Waves on the Beach, Meditate.
The wind's at your back and all over your face.
Just like that a Splashing Typhoon,
The Eyes of Love consume,
before the next full Moon.
Doesn't have to be a Summer Day,
Love Walks in the Exact same way.
So let the truth unfold for 'Public Love,'
To have and to hold, with 'Kisses and Huggs."
The Sun is gone, it's All Set,
If you're with the Right One, have No Regrets.

The Early-Bird Special!

The 'Early-Bird' Gets The Worm...
And Everybody Else Gets His Leftovers!
In This World Of Today's Employee High Turnover.
He Who Gets There 1st Gets The Pick Of The Litter.
While 'Johnny Came Lately' Stays Angry And Bitter.
The Earlier, The Better Can Keep You At The Ready.
Over Time You Accumulate Bounty,
For Efforts Held Steady.
'Early-Bird' If You Dare, For A Price That Pays You Back.
You're Up Before 'The Break Of Dawn'
And Keeping Things On Track.
The Extra Effort Is Noticed When Promotions Are Made.
When, Responsible Leaders Are Chosen For Upgrade.
Dedication And Determination Will Always Rule,
Owners Take Notice Of Those,
Ready To Blossom And Bloom.
Preparation And Accountability
Are How You Demonstrate.
So 'Early-Bird', You Can never get there Too Early,
Or Stay Too Late.
The Rewards Can Be Great! You Will Find It To Be True.
You Will Fill Your Nest As Always, A Blessing To You!
Blessing From 'Father-Time' For Your Extra Efforts.
Bringing Great Rewards For "The Early-Bird-Special!"

Just Next Them!

Just Next Them= When They're Moving Too Fast!
Just Next Them= When You Don't Do Back And Forth!
Just Next Them= When You're Only Allowed To Text Them!
Just Next Them= When They're Just Juggling Lovers!
Just Next Them= When It's All About Me!
Just Next Them= When They Smile Too Damn Much!
Just Next Them= When They're A Habitual Liar!
Just Next Them= When You're Constantly Holding Their Hand!
Just Next Them= When You have To Chase Down Your Money!
Just Next Them= When They Keep Looking At Your Friend!
Just Next Them= When They keep It To Themselves!
Just Next Them= When They're Needy All The Time!
Just Next Them= When They Keep Committing Those Crimes!
Just Next Them= When All They Do Is Complain!
Just Next Them= When They Ask For A Favor and Don't Know You!

"Beware Of The Scammer!"

Treat Me Good

None Kinder more Courteous With Open Arms For Some,
Some Kinds Of Love Has Spirit, That's Not For Everyone.
You All Get A Smile and A Wish For Better Days,
But What's Close To The Heart, Only Has So Much Space.
Be There For Me, I'll Be there Twice,
Make Love To Me, I Can Go All Night.
Some Loves You Can Teach How To Sustain,
Mine Comes All Natural, No Pressure On The Brain.
No Special Occasion Needed,
Gifts and Roses Are My Pleasure.
It's Not Going Out Of The Way,
To Set A Romantic Moment At The End of The Day.
The Kind Of Love That's Unconditional From The Start,
Doing Sweet and Silly Things, That Tug At The Heart.
'Treat Me Good and I'll Treat You Better',
Right From The Start, If It's You That I Treasure.
Acts of Reward For Us To Build An Empire of Comfort,
From The Business We Accomplish,
no need To Sound The Trumpet.
What's Special About Romantic Is,
It's A Sign of True Love.
Knowing What That Is, Is What You're Capable Of.

Puppies And Wolves
("Fangs")

A Puppy at Heart with A Werewolf Demeanor,
'Fangs' is Loyal To Compassion.
Showing up just in Time,
because She Loves Slaying The Dragon.
When Wolves move in for the thrill,
'Fangs' rushes through and spoiled their Kill.
Wolves feed off All that stands in their way,
Just for the Sport of it, they Devour their Prey.
Cages were made to Temper the Beast,
In This Jungle of ours they get to Roam Free.
So every time these Wolves get out of hand,
'Fangs' Swoops down and takes Command.
By giving back to The World Life's Harmony,
Where 'Werewolves' fade and 'Puppies' run Free.
Only A few in this Jungle has the Juice,
It takes 'Fangs' to stop a Bellowing Wolf.
Like A 'Saber-Tooth-Tiger' manning his fleet,
'Fangs' does the same while serving up defeat.
Another Hero legend, casted in the Perils of Time,
The Crowd's cheering, the Buzz Ends with a Bang!
For the Love shown and applause given,
for the Wolf-Dog named 'Fangs'.

Life's Lessons

Magic Hands and Strong Minds,
Calculated Thoughts in Fast Times.
Nothing Ventured Nothing Gained,
in Modern Times and Fast Lanes.
Learning Something New Every Day
or A Day Wasted with Nothing to Say.
Seeking Knowledge from 'The Cradle To The Grave',
Fighting Stone-Age problems, in A 'Man-Cave'.
A Mistake doesn't become an Error
until We Fail to Correct It,
A Time Sensitive Challenge in A World That's Hectic.
Part of The Solution Comes from The Problem,
Solutions and Resolutions
for Bright Minds To Solve Them.
Life's Lessons are Sometimes Borrowed,
Patents and Ideas Creates Our World of Tomorrow.
Doesn't Matter, Another Problem Solved,
To The Team or The ones Involved.
An Honorable Mention,
While Solving Life's Problems Comes Invention.
The Best Inventions Ever Made
Came From Oppression and Intention.
Some of The Greatest Lessons in Life Caused Sorrow,
That can Be Learned To Make Life Better
for Today and Tomorrow.

Raping Men's Pockets!

Counting The Money To Taste The Honey
They Celebrate with 'Bottled-Rockets',
These Women Don't Want No Man,
They want what's In His Pockets.
Jezebel Gave Them 'HELL' Putting A Price Tag On Desire,
She Ruled The Land With A Ruthless Hand,
Until She Caught Fire!
Where's the "Good-Wife' for Life, A Stripper in A Club?
Or The 2nd Tier, "Buy Me A Beer',
I'm Not In This for Love".
There's No Love To This Push and Shove,
Especially At Night,
The Smiles, Beauty and charm
Ruled By Their Own Device.
Stripped and Clad In Underwear, Ready For A Date,
Easing Through Pockets Is The Game They Love to Play.
So The Men Line Up Like Pitt-Bulls, With Their Pockets Full.
She Rides Them All Until It's A Lock,
Until He Wakes up In Shock!
'GOD' Given Beauty Meant For Man To Enjoy,
Now He's Being Treated Like Their Favorite Toy.
Love Went Out the Window Just like 'Jezebel'.
A Price Put On Pleasure and Joy,
Now They're Catching 'HELL!'
Worshipping The 'Sex God', That's Never Been Tamed.
They're 'Raping Men's Pockets' for the 'Bottled Rockets',
It's All In The Game.
When That Champagne Top Shots Off
and That 'Bottled Rocket' Gets Lost.
Can't Put That Corkscrew Back On At Whatever The Cost.
For Certain Kinds of Women There's No Stopping,
When It Comes To
Tasting The Honey For 'Bottled Rockets'.

New Year's Resolution!

Far Away From Those That I Love
I Was Surrounded By 'Fake-Friends,
The Worst Christmas I Ever had,
And I Swear It'll Never Happen Again.
A Reason For The Season
Brought On This Resolution.
It Will Be A Cold Day In Hell!
Before I Break This Constitution.
We All Must Enjoy The Moment,
Where ever Our Feet may Land.
The Thing Is Though,
You Never Let Anyone Alter The Plan.
The 'King's On Top and The Joy Never Stops.
While Joy Rains Down On Us All,
The Spirit Of Giving And Thanks To Be Living,
Let Your Spirit Answer The Call.

The Lone Warrior

The Lone-Warrior... His Army Was Killed!
The Infiltrators Raged and Tested His Will.
Battling Life's Problems To Bring Better Days,
For The Ears That's Shut and The Eyes That Raised!
Never Realizing That Warriors Are Born For Battle.
Battle-Tested To Embrace Death And Never Unravel.
Like Trying To Penetrate Steel As A Whole.
The Arena of Death Don't Score TKO's.
Knives In A Gun Fight Wears Thin,
The Warrior's Mold Is Projected To Win.
It Doesn't Matter The Condition
Or Level Of Balance,
A War-Torn Veteran Will Accept The Challenge.
Step On The Field Of Battle, Not Behind The Wall,
No Cowards Left Standing When Warriors Ball.

"Battle-Tested!"

Drug Dealers Beware!

Drug Dealers Lying On The Sidewalks
Bleeding And Left For Dead.
Not A Tear Was Shed, People Were Glad.
Now Put That In A Rap Song,
That Justice Was Served,
They're Not Coming Home.
Drug Dealers Shot Down Like A Dog In The Streets,
Female Assassins Are Bringing The Heat!
Recruited And Trained, 'The Real Police!'
Bodies Thrown In Manila Bay,
You Must Treat A Barbarian In A Barbarian Way!
American Drug Dealers,
That Brag About "Big Dollars!"
If They Only Knew How Lucky They Are,
They'd Be On Their Knees Tomorrow!
Destroying Families and say, "It's All In The Game!"
They'd Be thrown In Manila Bay
Without Fortune And Fame!
With The Roar Of Crowd Approval
In The Philippines.
While They Light Cigars and Drink Champagne.
'Drug Dealers Beware!'...
Where You Pay For Your Crimes And No One Is Spared!

The Tattoo Blues & Piercing Pains!

It's 'The Tattoo Blues And Piercing Pains',
Who You Represent Just Shout your Name!
Tats On Her Check Bone Legs And Thighs,
Piercing Pains Makes My nature Rise.
'Baby-Cakes', About To Drive Me Nuts!
She's Got A Tattoo Written On Her Butt.
It's The Tattoo Blues That Calls Our Names,
We're The Kings And Queens Of Piercing Pains!
A Symbol Of Our Love, A Symbol Of Our Pain,
Test Our Loyalty And Feel The Strain!
Sex You Up And Take You For A Trip.
They Got Pierced Up Eyes, Ears And Lips.
A Spiked Up Tongue And A Nipple Cradle,
A Diamond Pendant Pinned To Their Naval!
Studded-Nails Do You Like Toe-Rings,
Garter-Belts And Leather Things?
We All Started Out Riding Bikes And Chains,
And Now we're Living Under Just Our Names.
Don't Need No Drugs To Feel Our Pain,
Or To Celebrate A Victory In Our Names.
We're The Kings And Queens Of Piercing Pains!

Good N A Bad Way!

Friends= Good N A Bad Way!= Some for a day, a month, a year, a Lifetime!...2-catagories: Real & Fake!

Weed= Good N A Bad Way!= you can smoke it or consume it. The body was 'Not' built to consume 'smoke' but in this case it... Fights Cancer Cells; supposedly. Clouds The Mind.

Sex= Good N A Bad Way!= Doesn't matter with whom or how many. The Good= Feeling It. The Bad= The results can get Ugly. The Ugly= Fill in the blank_____

Knowledge= Good N A bad Way!= Great when used in the Positive. Bad= Disaster in a Brain-washed Cult; Nobody wins.

Beauty= Good N A Bad Way!= "Easy on the eyes". Beauty is really Skin Deep. All-Star Talent and Personality is A Thing Of Beautiful.

Money= Good N A bad Way!= Unlimited Power. Buy Anything, Do as you Please...The Negative= A lot of Country's Currency has Little Value where others have Great Value. The Root of all Evil. Crime!

Race= Good N A bad Way!= Color-Proud. Leads to Infatuation and Division. Mixed, Human= All one in the same, None better Than the other.

(Continues On Next Page)

Fire= Good N A Bad Way!= A lot of Great uses. The Good= Cooking, heating, Lighting, etc. The Bad= Can cause Injury and damage.

Sports= Good N A Bad Way!= To be Champion! Goals-Greatest of All Time! The Good= Money, Fun, Exercise. The Bad= Ego, Father-Time, Injuries is not a friend. Can be Fatal.

Paradise= Good N a bad Way!= Beautiful Places: White-Sand-Beaches, Palm-Trees, Blue-Skies. The Good= Life of Luxury. Petting, Pampering, Servants and Catering. The Bad= Very Expensive, Lots of Poverty Areas.

"There's always something Good in something someone thinks is Bad, and there's always something Bad in something someone thinks is Good."

"Good N A Bad Way!= The Big 10

SECTION III
Bonus Extras

Poetic-Jingles & Songs

Castles In The Sand
(Pure Harmony Song)

Castles in the sand...
Ooh Baby, won't you take my hand.
Lead the way for better days,
We can't go wrong, on A Love Song.

Castles in the sand...
Ooh Baby, sunset with a Tan.
You can rest assure,
Here's the cure, we've been hoping for.

Castles in the sand...
Ooh Baby, won't you take my hand.
It's how much I need you here,
Ooh Baby, make it Crystal Clear.
Lead the way for better days,
We can't go wrong, on A Love Song.

A Castle in the sand, we've been hoping for...
Won't you take my hand, Love on the Seashore...
Castles, Castles, Castles....talking bout Castles...
Castles! Oooh!

Curtains Of Love
(Song-Version "Tugging At My Heart")

Like Love in a magic Show,
Puppets on a string,
It's more than Smoke & Mirrors,
When it's a beautiful thing.

That Background Sound,
Keeps holding me down,
Won't you please help me,
With this All Natural Thing.

Main Chorus: Curtains Of Love

      Won't you help me,
      Tugging at my Heart
      Keeps pulling apart,
      I'm Addicted.

That background Sound
Keeps holding me down,
Won't you please help me.

2nd Chorus: Curtains of Love
      Tugging at my Heart,
      I'm Addicted.

Final Verse:
Tugging at my Heart,
You keep pulling apart
    I'm Addicted.

For The Lover In You,
It's The Curtains Of
      Love,
We're Addicted!

All To The Good!
(Song & Poem)

Main Chorus: All To The Good...This Is Something That's Understood!
> A Little Something Just For You,
> I Know You Wonder How I Knew.
> Something To Help Pull You Through,
> From The Heart I Heard You.

2nd Chorus: The LORD Said It, You Must Have Read It, The LORD Said It.
> Keep The Faith And Stay On Track,
> It's Not Just ME That Has Your Back,
> Wonder Where Your Meals Come From,
> I Feed The Birds And Made The Sun.

Main Chorus: All To The Good...This Is Something That's Understood!
2nd Chorus: The LORD Said It, You Must Have Read It, The LORD Said It.
> I Watched You Take Your 1st Step,
> I'll Be There At Your Last Breath.
> I Put You In "THE BOOK Of LIFE",
> On MY 'Guest-List' For Paradise.

(Continues On Next Page)

2nd Chorus: The LORD Said It, You Must Have Read It, The LORD Said It.
Main Chorus: All To The Good...This Is Something That's Understood!

> I Know You Can't Go It Alone,
> The Miracle's MINE To Lead You Home.
> Gave You Wisdom When You Had Doubt,
> The 'Fruit Of The Spirit' Brought About.
> The Results Are Final That Just Came In,
> I'm Not Surprised I Made the Wind.

I'll Calm The Storm Before It Can Blow,
> I Made The Gardens And Rivers Flow.

2nd Chorus: The LORD Said It, You Must Have Read It, The LORD Said It.
> Hey LORD!... Thank You LORD You Pulled Me Through...
> Hey LORD!... I'm So Glad... That I Found You.
> All To The Good...This Is Something That's Understood!
> The LORD Said It, You Must Have Read It, The LORD Said It.
NOTE: Repeat 2nd Chorus= 3-Times No-Music...All Harmony!

(The End).

Someone Like That!
(A Tribute To MJ)

Where You Gone Get Someone Like That,
Guaranteed Or Your Money Back!

All Broke Down In His Favorite Hat,
Who Moves Like That, Dance Like That?
Guaranteed Or Your Money Back!

Where You Gone get Someone Who Sings Like That,
In A Groove Like That, Silky-Smooth Can You Bring That Back!

Main Chorus: Show Me What You've Been Missin,
               I Need Your Huggs & Kissin,
               The Moon-Dancer, The Moon-Walker.

Where You Gone Get One Like That,
With An Unmatched Spirit, That Was Fun Like That!
Guaranteed or Your money back!

Who Kept It Brand-New, With A Groove Like That.
Around The World And HE Doubled-Back!
Smooth Like That, Can You Bring That Back!
Guaranteed Or Your Money Back!

Main Chorus: Show Me What You've Been Missin,
               I Need Your Huggs & Kissin.
               The Moon-Dancer, The Moon-Walker.

"Tribute To MJ" Reggae-Styled (Vocal Only!), Party Song.

Coconut Rum!

Main Chorus:
 Foot-Prints In The Sand
 The Sky Be Holding My Hand,
Sippin On Coconut Rum
 Out There Under The Sun.

Main Chorus (Cont):
Foot-Prints In The Sand
The Sky Be
Holding my Hand.
Sippin On Coconut Rum
Out There Under the Sun!

Ocean Water So Blue
Bringing Out The Flavor In You!

We're Having So Much Fun,
Sippin On Coconut Rum!

2nd Chorus:
Foot-Prints In The Sand
The Sky Be Holding my Hand.

Luv That Coconut Rum
We Be Havin Fun,
Out There
Under The Sun,

Beach House Under The Sun
Drinking That Coconut Rum.

Until The Break Of Dawn.

Beach-Tracks In The Sand,
The Sky Be Holding Our Hands!

.

Bouncing That Bum, Bum, Bum!
Out There Having Fun!
Keep Holding Up That Cup
We'll Be Cranking it Up!

(Song-Ends!).

Show Me Where GOD'S At?
(Poem & Song)

Main Chorus: "Show Me Where GOD'S At?
           All The Biblical Scholars Just Drew Us A Map."
           It's Revealed In The Secret Scrolls
.   And The Seven Seals,
           A Miracle, Heavenly Bound For The Spiritual.

Main Chorus: "Show Me Where GOD'S At?
  (Twice)   The Biblical Scholars Just Drew Us A Map."
           Good Deeds, Let The Light Shine Through
           On Those In Need.
           Confused? From The Pain & Suffering.
           By Me And You.

Main Chorus: "Show Me Where GOD'S At?
All The Biblical Scholars Just Drew Us A Map."
It's Revealed In The Secret Scrolls & The Seven Seals,
A Miracle, Heavenly Bound For The Spiritual.
Is It Sealed, Truth Of The Matter Will Be Revealed.
Have You Heard, 'The Chosen Few' Gave Us The Word.

Main Chorus: "Show Me Where GOD'S At?
           The Biblical Scholars Just Drew Me A Map."
     Keep The Faith,
     The LORD Loves Those Who Appreciate.
     A Journey's End, GOD Brought It All Back Again.

(Continues On Next Page)

Main Chorus: "Show Me Where GOD's At?
The Biblical Scholars Just Drew Us A Map."
A Miracle, Heavenly Bound For The Spiritual,
"The Heavenly KING!"...
Trust In 'HIS' Word When 'HE' Intervenes.

Main Chorus: "Show Me Where GOD's At?
The Biblical Scholars Just Drew Us A Map."

(Song-Ends!).

All In!
(Poem & Song)

Main Chorus: All In!...When You Lock 1 Door Another 1 Opens,
That Opens The Senses, That Keeps You Scopin.

        Bad-Boy= You like To play With Toys,
        Bad-Boy= Roll Over, And Give Me More.
        Bad-Girl= You Think You own The World,
        Bad-Girl= Roll Over, like a Little Girl.

Main Chorus: All In!...When You Lock 1 Door Another 1 Opens,
That Opens The Senses, That keeps You Scopin.

        Bad-Girl= You Say It's All About Me,
        Bad-Girl= Roll Over, Life's A Travesty.
        Bad-Boy= You Like To Have Your way,
        Bad-Boy= Roll Over, To a Brand-New Day.

Main Chorus=   All In!...When You Lock 1 Door Another 1
Opens, That Opens The Senses, That keeps You Scopin'.

        Bad-Boy= You Say It's On And Poppin!
        Bad-Boy= Roll Over, This Club Ain't Hoppin!
        Bad-Girl= All You Do Is Celebrate,
        Bad-Girl= Bad News Headed Your Way!

        You Think It's All About You, = Bad-Boy!
        What You Gonna do.... = Bad-Girl!
        ...Playing The fool!... = Bad-Boy, Bad-Girl!

Extended-Version: Bad-Boy!= You Like To Play.
                  Bad-Boy!= What'll You Say!
                  Bad-Girl!= You Rule The World,
                  Bad-Girl!= What'll You Say!

                  (Song-Ends!).

My Own Plan

Main Chorus: "I Got My Own Plan Man, My Own Plan Man
       Oooh, I Got My Own Plan man."
       No Controversy, I Got my Own Plan Man!
       I Know You Heard Me, Got My Own Plan Man!
       I'm On A Mission, Got My Own Plan Man!
       Where's The Competition, Got My Own Plan Man!

Main Chorus: "Oooh, Me Got My Own Plan Man,
       Oooh, Me Got My Own Plan Man."
       Start My Own Production, Got My Own Plan Man!
       What's The Seduction, Got My Own Plan Man!
       Progress Intended, I Got My Own Plan Man!
       Don't Get Offended, Got My Own Plan Man!

Main Chorus: "Oooh,Me Got My Own Plan Man,
       Oooh, Me Got My Own Plan Man."
       From Jamaica To London, Got My Own Plan Man!
       Success Is A Coming, Got My Own Plan Man!
       All The way To Havana, Got My Own Plan Man!
       Don't Go Bananas, I Got My Own Plan Man!

Main Chorus: "Oooh, Me Got My Own Plan Man!
       Oooh, Me Got My Own Plan Man!
       Contagious Not Outrageous, Got My Own Plan man!
       Don't Contaminate It, Got My Own Plan Man!
       No Doubt About It, Got My Own Plan Man!
       I'm Gone Scream & Shout It, Got My Own Plan Man!
       Just Call Me Later, I Got My Own Plan Man!
       Down By The Equator, I Got My Own Plan Man!

(Song Ends!)..."The Plan!".

Treat Me Good

Main Chorus:
>Treat me Good
>And you'll Never Regret It,
>Life's So Good
>And You Never Have To Sweat It.

Mini Chorus:
>Volunteer's up!
>All You Need In Life, Turned Up!
>Volunteer's Up!
>Cream Of The Crop And It Don't stop!
>Volunteer's Up!
>Give It To You, Til You Get Enough.

Main Chorus:
>Treat Me Good
>And You'll Never Regret It,
>Life's So Good
>And You Never Have To Sweat It.

Mini Chorus:
>Volunteer's Up!
>All You Need In Life, Turned Up!
>Volunteer's Up!
>Give It To You,
>Til You Get Enough.

Final Verse: (Concludes).
>Dream Cups!
>Have a Sip & You Won't Give Up!
>This Cup Of Dreams Is A Beautiful Thing.

(Song-Ends)

Proud Out Loud!
(Song & Poem)

GOD Gave You To Me...
And I'm Proud Out Loud, Proud Out Loud!

GOD Saved You For Me...
And I'm Proud Out Loud, Proud Out Loud!

HE Set Us Free!...
And I'm Proud Out Loud, Proud Out Loud!

You Gave Your Hand To Me...
And I'm Proud Out Loud, Proud Out Loud!

Our Love Will Forever Be...
And I'm Proud out Loud, Proud Out Loud!

Only You Can Make Me Smile...
Proud Out Loud, Proud out Loud!

Please Don't Ever Leave...
Proud Out Loud, Proud Out Loud!
Chorus Sing!..."Proud Out Loud, Proud Out Loud!

Beat Around The Bush!

Main Chorus: "Yabba Dabba Dang! No! Do! Do!
    What Does It Take , To Get the Truth Out Of You!"

Dippin In The Mustard And Can't Catch Up!
    Forget The Chit-Chatter, We've Had Enough!
    Something Went down The Wrong Way.
    When We Asked You, You Got Nothing To say!
    Talk about Keeping It real, Can You Make It Plain,
    Get to The Point, Yabba Dabba Dang!

Mini Chorus: "Get To The Point Point Point,
    And Make It Plain Plain Plain."

No Candy-Coated, Fabricated, Mellow-Dramatic Cush,   . Don't
Waste Time Beating Around The Bush!
  Long-Winded Speeches We Don't Need,
  Just Keep It Real, If You Don't Mind Please.
  Forget The Chit-chatter, Because The Rest Don't matter,
   No Need To Serve It Up, On A Silver Platter!

Main Chorus: " Dang! Yabba Dabba, And No! Do1 Do!
    What Does It Take, To Get The Truth Out Of You!"

Mini Chorus: "Get To The Point Point Point,
    And Make It Plain Plain Plain."
    You Got Your Bachelors, Masters And Your PHD,
    Just More Of This Piled High And Deep!
    Get To The Point, And Make It Plain,

(Continues On Next Page)

When The Public Thinks, You're Playing A Game.
It Took Forever For You To Spit It Out.
Now You're Going On Forever,
Just Running Your Mouth.

Main Chorus: " Yabba Dabba Dang! And No1 Do1 Do!
What Does It Take, To Get The Truth out Of You!

"Truthalicious!"...(Song Ends!).

Pay Me!
(Hip Hop Song)

Pay Me!...All Of My Damn Money!
Pay Me!...Ain't A Damn Thing Funny!
Pay Me!...If I Catch You That Azz Is Mine!
Pay Me!...Get It Right This Time!
I Shouldn't Have To Go Through This Every Single Time!
Pay Me!...I Shouldn't Have To Ask You Again.
Pay Me!...You Spoil Friendship When you Loan To a
Friend!
Pay Me!...For my Talents And my Skills!
Pay Me!...For breaking My Back At the Mill!
Pay Me!...For Giving You All Of Those Thrills!
Pay Me!...She Left It All In Her Will!
Now You're Holding Back, Pay Me! What's The Deal?
Pay Me!...Bill Collectors On My Back.
Pay Me!...I'm Trying To Get Stacked!
I'm Out There Getting It Everyday...Pay Me!
My 'Homie' I Don't Play!...Pay Me!

SECTION IV

Bonus-Extras

Poetic Stories

"THE BLACK SHEEP SOLDIERS!"

EXCEPTIONAL HEROES DEDICATED TO PROTECTING THE MINORITY WITH TACT AND CLASS. THEIR UNTIRING EFFORTS TO HELP OTHERS IS UNMATCHED AND THEY ALWAYS GET THE JOB DONE. CONSIDER YOUR PROBLEM SOLVED WHEN YOU REACH OUT TO 'THE BLACK SHEEP SOLDIERS!' IN "YOU AIN'T WHITE ENOUGH!".

SO, I INTRODUCE TO YOU THE NEW WAVE OF 'SUPER-HEROES' IN MY 'BAD-HAIR-DAYS!' & 'TALES FROM THE HIP!' COLLECTION...GOD BLESS!

The King Of Clean
(The Laundry Wizard)

A Chicago Dry-Cleaner, Who Started With One Store,
Who Rose Up To Have Many By Striving For More.
A Lot Of Hard Work While Giving Up The Fun,
He Eventually Named One of Them, After One Of His Sons.
Specializing In Cleaning Took On A Whole New Meaning,
Long Before "The Jefferson's", It's True No Dreaming!
Loyal Customers For Decades Gave Nothing But Praise,
For Providing Such Good Service, Back In Those Days.
For A Dedicated Man Who Put In The Work,
Moving On Up To Open More Stores,
The 'Bubbled-Ceiling' He Burst!
Now Another Thankless Job That's Hardly Recognizable,
Cleaning Dirty Laundry Is now A Billion Dollar Business
Around The Globe.
A Father's Choice Of Business And He Did It Well,
With Lots Of Hard Work And Stories To Tell.
Taught Us Business Work Ethics
And Putting The Customer First,
A Formula For Winning When Dispensing The Dirt.
The "Laundry-Wizard" Has Passed On And Although It Hurt.
He was "The King Of Clean" In Chicago, And One Of The First.
He Did Something That We Can All Be Proud Of,
By Making Something From Nothing And Showing Some Love.

NOTE: "Tales From The Hip!" & " Bad-Hair Days!" Collection.

Cats, Rats & Candles
(Mrs. Weedermire)

After Telling On All Of His Friends. To Clear Away The Competition For His Burglary Schemes, "Lucky The Burglar", Moved In On 'Mrs. Weedermire's Manson. Intent, On Stealing Her Priceless Jewelry Collection, Stored In Her Safe, Located In Her Study; 'Lucky' Moved In For The Kill!

Mrs. Weedermire Had A Devout Affinity For 'Cats & Candles'. Which She Kept Lit Nightly, Leaving them To Burn All Night, To Ward Off Evil Spirits. "Miles", Her Cat Observed "Lucky The Burglar" Coming In Through A Window. As He Lay Resting On A Window-Seal, Nearby. "Miles" Ready to Tell, Ran Recklessly And Fled Upstairs To Warn 'Mrs. Weedermire'. Knocking Over Candles Along The Way. Igniting The Curtains In The Hall And Bedroom To Flames.

Meanwhile, The Smoking-Mad, Chain-Smoking Cat-Burglar Downstairs Got Frustrated And Was Unable To Open The Safe. Angrily He Thumped His Lit Cigarette To The Carpet, As He Stood Up. He Knocked Over 'Mrs. Weedermire's' Antique Lantern, On Her Study-Desk.

The Noise Woke 'Mrs. Weedermire'. As "Miles" Sat On Her Chest, While Licking Her Face. The Crash Of The Lantern Ignited a Fire In The Study From The Lit Cigarette. Hearing The Screaming For 'Help' Upstairs, As 'Mrs. Weedermire Saw The Flames & Smoke. "Lucky The Burglar" Decided To Abandon His Craft And Escaped Through The Window From Which He Came.

Once Outside, He Raced Away. Looking Back, He Noticed The 2-Fires. The One Upstairs Was A Mystery, But The One Downstairs In The Study Had To Be His. Considering Himself Lucky, He Disappeared Into The Brush. Running Like A 'Madman'.

(Continued On Next Page)

Meanwhile, Mrs. Weedermire Took 'Miles' Into Her Arms And Headed For The Stairs. With The House A Blaze, In Haste, She Raced Down The Stairs. Trying To Save 'Miles,' Just Before Her House Burned To The Ground.

About Half Way Down, She Stumbled And Fell. Sending 'Miles' Flying Into The Flames! After Taking A Hard Fall And Breaking A Leg, From The Tumbling. She Managed To Crawl And Open The Front Door.

As She Made It Outside, 'Miles' Came Blazing By With His Hair On Fire, But Still Alive! He Rolled On The Lawn To Smother The Flames. 'Mrs. Weedermire' Got Close Enough To Throw Dirt On 'Miles'. Helping To Put Out The Fire.

By Now Someone had Noticed The Spectacle Of A Burning House And Called For Help. As The Fire-Trucks Raced To Rescue The Remnants From The Fire. 'Lucky', Still On The Move In The Brush. And Refusing To Be Seen Or Come Up For Air. Seeking Refuge And Peace From All The Noise. Got More Than He Bargained For. When He Forgot To Look Both Ways, When He Ran Out Onto The Highway. A Fire-Truck Running Late For The Scene. Hit Him Head On. Killing Him, Instantly!

Back At What Was Left Of The Mansion. A Fireman Took A Towel And Rubbed "Miles" Down. And Handed Him To 'Mrs. Weedermire'. She Peeled Back The Towel, To Find 'Miles' Had Become The 1st Ball-Headed Cat. Who Now looked Like A Rat; Only Too Long And Not So Fat. 'Mrs. Weedermire' Kissed 'Miles'. Reached Into Her Housecoat Pocket, Pulled Out A Candle And Tickled 'Miles'...On The Ground Where The Window Use To Be, That The Cat-Burglar Used. Sat A Deck Of Cards: "His Lucky Deck."

Excerpt From: "Bad Hair Days!" & "Tales From The Hip!" Collection.

Sweet Air Lane!
(Tales From The Hip!)

A Party Has Always Been A Playground For Adults. An Atmosphere To Release Frustration: "No Need To Mob Up!"... "A Chill Zone." With All The Elements: Cock-Out-The Food Was Bangin! -, Card-Party, And The 'Sounds' (Music)...On Blast! Let's Not Forget The Sounds, The-1's & 2's...Bumpin With That 'Old-School' Flavor & 'New-School' Beats! Thumpin That Shake, Rattle & Stroll-Music.

It Got So Good They Started Out, 'Steppin' Chicago-Style. Then They Let It All Hang Loose. 'Stucky' Started Tossing Women In The Air, Like A Chef Tossing Salad. And, Set It Off With Petite 'Lady-Z'. She Was Just The Right Size, As 'Stucky' Caught Her By Surprise: 'Up-Sidaisy-Whee!'. It Was On & Poppin! And It Got Good!

'Stucky's Aunt 'Bella' Sitting At The Card-Table With Her Crew And Observing. Laughed Until She Cried! 'Lady-Z', Who Thought It Was Cute, But Insisted That 'Stucky' Stop! 'Stucky' Unable To Resist Or Freeze His Moves, Gave Into Temptation And Kept Hittin It With 'Lady-Z'. Up Again She Went. 'Up-Sidaisy-Whee!', Tossing Her By
The Hip-Catch Her By The Hip Rhythm, Like In A Broadway Show.

All Eyes On Them: 'Ups-Sidaisy-Whee!'. It Caught On Like 'Tarzan On The Vine'. The Madness And Gladness Was Contagious Spreading Like Wild-Fire. The Party was Fully-Crunk! Everybody was Lit, Bottoms-Up & Tossing Cups. Partners Were Flying In The Air Everywhere!

(Continued On Next Page)

It Was Raining Women On 'Sweet Air Lane!' Most Of The women Anyway. There Were A Few Who Couldn't Be Lifted. They Showed Them Love Too. As 'Lady-Z' Danced Around In The Air. Now Of Her Own Free Will. Able To 'High-5' With The Other Honey's, Like A Brother On A Slam-Dunk!

Now 'Big-Bertha' Got In On The Fun! And Started Tossing Her Man, 'Fragile-Rock', Also Known As 'Slim-Goody'. Up! With the Women He Went. 'Betty-Boo', Brenda-Boo' And 'Lady-Sue' Just To Name A Few. 'Ups-Sidaisy-Whee!.' 'Fragile-Rock' Didn't Like It But 'Big-Bertha' Did It Anyway. 'Fragile-Rock' Showed Some Love And Started 'High-5-ing' The Ladies In Mid-Air.

Hair Was Flying Everywhere. A Loose Braid Hit 'Buddy-B' In The Face But He Kept It Movin, With A Smile. 'Buddy-B' Tossed 'Bubbles' Up And As She Came Down, She Got Missed! Nothing Serious. She Just Stubbed Her Toe. Back To The Sky 'Bubbles' Went Reaching For a 'Halo'.

The Women Landed In The Arms Of The "Magic On Sweet Air Lane." At The Same Time Someone Yelled! "Time To Eat!". Without Hesitation Or Excuses The Women Took Off Like 'Delta Airlines', And Beat The Men To The Food. The Brothers Were Still Catching Their Breath From The Workout.

But, One Brother From Another Mother, Beat Them All! The Leader Of The Pack 'Stucky' Caught 'Lady-Z', Whipped Her Into A Spin And Took Off! When, The Ladies Invaded 'The Party-Buffet'. 'Stucky' Was Sitting At The Table, Polishing Off A Full-Plate Of Ribs. The Ladies Smiled And Shook Their Heads.

'Stucky' Winked With A Mouth Full Of Food. The Mad-Scents From The Flavor-Rich-Food, Could Be Smelled All Over 'Sweet-Air-Lane!' With The Jazzed-Up Sound Of Music Ringing In Your Ear, And A Background Of Crunch, Crunch, Smack, Smack! They Ate Their Backs Out! And, Got Plates To Go!

(Continued On Next Page)

As They Headed For The Door. They All Only Had One Question: 'When Can We Do It Again, On 'Sweet-Air-Lane?!'

Excerpt From: "Bad Hair Days!' & "Tales From The Hip!" Collection.

(Based On A True Story).

Bonnie & Pride
(Bad Hair Days)

'Pride' Woke Up! Some Of His Hair Fell Out. On His Way To The Bathroom, He Bumped Into The Door And Lost A Tooth. "DAMN!", Was This Day Starting Out Bad! The Suit 'Pride' Had Laid Out The Night Before, Had A Bad Stain On It. Oh Well, He Just Grabbed Another One. His Favorite Suit Ruined! How Did That Happen? He Frowned. Determined Not To Let That Spoil His Day.

As He Moved Along Fully Dressed, About To Head Out The Door. He Reached For His Briefcase, And The Handle Came Off. "DAMN!" To Add Insult To Injury, Little Did He Know. The Suit He Was Wearing Had A Hole In The Back Pocket Of His Pants. And So, As He Bent Down And Arm-Wrapped His Briefcase. Unbeknown, His Wallet fell To The Floor. As He Headed Out The Door. Leaving His Wallet Behind.

Concentrating On His Next Move... As He Got Into His Old-Beat-Up 'Hoopty' And Turned The Key. "DAMN!" It Wouldn't Start. Looking Up And Seeing His Neighbor, 'Bobby Upshaw'. Thinking Quickly. 'Pride' Flagged Him Down, With His Jumper-Cables In Hand. And Got Himself A Jump-Off.

He Smiled To Himself. As His Junk-Buggy Blew Grey Smoke Going Down The Highway. 'Pride ' Turned On The Radio And The Music Was Bumpin And Poppin. He Thought About 'Bonnie' His Girl-Friend. Who Had Dumped Him For Being Late, For A Love Connection Concert In Hidden Hills Gardens. By The Time They Got There The Concert Was Over. It Wasn't His Fault, Car Trouble As Usual.

Well, 'Pride' Was About To Upgrade. He'd Just Gotten A New Job. And Today Was His 1st Day. Things Were Looking Up!

(Continued On Next Page)

He Was Absolutely Certain. "Bonnie" Would Be Back. After All, Time Heals all Wounds. With The New Job And Full-Time Classes, He'd Be Back And On His Way. As He Rounded The Bend. Nothing Could Be Further From The Truth...

'Bonnie' Was Still Mad At "Pride'. But He Was Awfully Handsome, Smart And Easy On The Ears. Most Guys Bugged Her, With Their Macho-Egotistical Attitudes. 'Pride' Had Flavor & Rhythm. Plus, He was Kind, Funny And Considerate. A Little Bit On The Late Side, But Nobody's Perfect. She Liked Him And Sometimes She Liked Him A lot. "Oh, Why Don't He Get Himself A Reliable Car. And, Get Rid Of That Junk-Buggy!" Reasonably Thinking. " I Know Education Is Number One. And, All Good Things Comes To Those Who Wait. But, That Thing Is A Total Embarrassment. Oh Well, I Forgive Him. He's Been Calling And Begging For Days. I Love You Too, My Poetic Unadulterated Genius."

Thinking Back,... She Woke Up! Her Hair Was Falling Out. Loose Strains Lay All Over her Pillow. On Her Way To The Bathroom, She Bumped Into The Door and Loosened A Tooth! "DAMN!", Was This Day Starting Out On A Bad Note.

'Bonnie' Favorite Dress had A Bad Stain On It. Oh Well, She Just Grabbed Another One. Her Favorite Dress Ruined! How Did That Happen? She Winced, Determined Not To Let It Bother Her.

As 'Bonnie' Moved Along, Fully Dressed. About, To Head Out The Door. She Reached For Her Laptop. The Side Hinges Popped Loose. The Base Fell To The floor, With A Loud Crashing Sound. And, She Was Left Holding The Screen. "DAMN!", My

(Continued On Next Page)

New Laptop. Oh My Goodness!" She Sat Down On The Sofa And Put It All Back Together. It Powered Up And Came Back On.

"Thank GOD." It's Still Under Warranty...They'll Just Have To Replace It. I Think I'll Get Through the Day. It Better!" She Slid It Into Her Black Cloth Carry Bag. Stood Up And Headed For The Door.

She Reached Over For Her Chain Handled Purse. And One End Popped Loose. "Oh! Not you Too!" She Cried. 'Bonnie' Managed To Clip The loose End To The Material. She Swung It Over Her Shoulder, And With The Tote-Bag In Hand, Jetted Out The Front Door.

Now In Her Car, Going Down The Highway, She Thought. "This Has Been One Hell Of A Morning. The Day Can't Get Any Worse Than This." 'Bonnie" Could Still Make Her Final Interview For The New Management Job. They Assured Her That Job Was Hers. "Just Don't Be Late," Was What They Said. Many Had Applied For the Job, More Qualified. But, They Wanted Someone Young And Energetic. However, They Were A Stickler For Time. "Oh, She Thought. 'Pride' Is Going To Be So Proud Of Me." As She Rounded The Bend, Nothing Could Be Further From The Truth...

As They Rounded The Bend, Nobody Saw It Coming. "Pride", Accidently Dropped A Lit Cigarette And Bent Down To Pick It Up. Swerving Across The Lane. "Bonnie", Was Trying To Put Her Favorite Earrings On. She Dropped One And Went To Pick It Up. Swerving Across The Lane. They Looked Up At The Same Time. Saw Each Other But It Was Too Late. A Head-On Collision That Threw Both Of Them Through The Windshield Into Each Others' Arms For the Last Time...

(Continued On Next Page)

...No New Job For "Pride', No New Promotion For "Bonnie", Just A "Bad Hair Day" Gone MAD! "Bonnie & Pride" Held Together In The Hereafter.

Excerpt From: "Bad Hair Days!" & "Tales From The Hip!" Collection.

Midnight Swim
(Bad Hair Days!)

One Night A Man Broke Into A Park Recreational Center, That Had An Outdoor Fenced-In Swimming Pool. His Eyes Bulged, When He Got Into The Storage Room. "Willie-The-Wino" Had Struck Gold! Plenty To Steal!

'Willie' Stacked Up Some 'Blu-Ray' Players, 2-Portable HD TV's, And A Big- Bag Of Accessories. On His Way To The Door, He Spotted A Big Brand New Beach-Towel, And Several Pairs Of Swimming Trunks. "Willie' Promptly Rolled Them Up In The Towel, And Stuffed It Under His Arm.

Feeling Good About His Score, And Everything Lined Up Outside, Ready To Go. 'Willie' Pulled Out A Pint Of Wine To Celebrate. After Devouring Over Half Of His Bottle. 'Willie-The-Wino' Was Ready To Start Hauling The Goods.

All Of A Sudden, 2-Thuggs Jumped Him. Beat Him Brutally, And Took All Of His Goods: Except The Towel. As They Fled, They Ran Right Into The Police, (5-Oh!). Who Had Answered The Silent-Alarm. They Took Them And The Merchandise Into Custody.

The Original Robber, Glad Fate Stepped In. Struggled To His Feet, Picking Up The Towel With Him. Eyes Swollen And Bleeding From The Mouth And Nose. He Headed In The Opposite Direction Towards The Pool.

Half-Way There, 2-Vicious Attack Dogs Came Out Of Nowhere! 'Willie-The-Wino' Found New Life! As He Sprinted To The Pool. The Fence Was Locked. So, He Dropped The Towel And Started Climbing. One Dog Jumped And Caught Him In The Butt: Rewarded With A Piece Of His Pants And Broken Skin. The Man Set 'A New!

(Continues On Next Page)

79

Olympic World Record' For Fence-Climbing! And Was Over In No Time! The Dogs Retreated As They Fought Over The Towel. Sprinkling Trunks All Over The Park As They Ran.

Suddenly, Some Gun-Shots Rang-Out! And, 'Willie' Immediately Jumped In The Pool. The Dogs Stopped Playing And Observed. A Man Was Chasing Another Man. Whom, Had Tried To Rob Him. The Victim Had Pulled Out His

Pistol, While Handing over The Loot! The Would-Be Robber Fled. Forgetting The Money, And So, Began The Chase. That Went Right By The Pool.

Meanwhile, 'Willie', The Original Robber, Who Had Jumped In The Pool For Safety. Forgot That He Couldn't Swim. Seeing The 2-Men Run By From Under The Water. He Was Ready To Come Up, But He Couldn't. 'Willie-The-Wino' Drowned! The Dogs Raced Away.

At The break Of Dawn, All That Was Found Was 'Willie'. And A Almost Empty Bottle of Wine, Floating Next To Each Other. A Big Hole In The Seat Of His Pants, Revealed A Bright Red Shiny Spot. Reflected By The Sun.

The Recreational Director, Ms. Chestnut Told The Police. Not Only Had They Been Robbed. But, They Found A Drunk Who Had Drowned. Who Evidently Fell On His Butt. And, Took A 'Midnight Swim.'

With News Of Their Own. The Police Informed The Director Of Another Body Found 500 Feet Away. Of A Man With A Ski-Mask Draped Half-Way over His Face, With 5-Fatal Gun Shot Wounds. Later Identified As 'Harry The Hippie.' A Suspected Foiled Robbery Attempt, With 'The Midnight-Swimmer' Being The Only Witness.

As, Another Unsolved Mystery Unfolded. The Officers Noticed The 2-Dogs Playing With The Beach Towel. As If On

(Continued On Next Page)

Cue, They Stopped. Sat-Up And Took Notice, And Started To Bark In Unison. The Officers Looked At Each Other. Then Back At The Dogs. Then In Unison They Said, "NaaH!".

While Shaking Their Heads And Walking Away. As They Climbed Into The Prowler. That Faced The Dogs. They Couldn't Help But Notice. The Dogs Were Still In Their Sitting Positions And still Barking At Them. As They Started To Drive off, The Barking Stopped! They Both Said It At The Same Time. "Let's Round Up The Usual Suspects." While, Both Were Thinking..."If Only Dogs Could Talk."

Excerpt From: "Bad Hair Days!" & "Tales From The Hip!" Collection.

You Ain't White Enough!
(The Big Payback!)

On This Special Day, The 100th Year Anniversary Of The "Klu-Klux-Klan". The 'Grand-Dragon' Was Set To Address His 'Brotheren'. Dressed In His White-Robe And Wearing His Crown. Standing Before A Packed Crowd, About To Deliver One Of His Award Winning Speeches, Before His Lilly-White Brotheren.

He Noticed Some Men Of Color, Standing In The back. All Wearing Long Black-Robes With Hoods And Wearing Dark Shades. Instantly, He Knew They Weren't Invited. They All Resembled The Bait For Execution Of Years Past And Today.

For The Distribution Of Hate, Chaos, Mayhem And Debauchery For American-Terrorism'. The Door Was Always Open And These Invaders Had Let Themselves In. Only A 'Pain-Freak' Would Walk Into The Lion's Den; Or A 'Foolish Warrior'. Sacrifices Had To Be Made, And Tonight's Celebration Was About To be Given A Bonus. The 'Grand-Dragon' Smiled At The Thought, Of Delivering A Full-Course-Meal With Dessert. This Was Definitely Going To Be A Historical Moment In 'Klu-Klux-Klan' History!

The Black Dressed Intruders. "The Black Sheep Soldiers" Were Made Up Of Minorities Of All Kinds: Blacks, Asian, American Indian, Jews, Italian And Hispanics. They All Came To Weather The Aged-Old-Storm Of Racism. And To Bring Peace And Love To The "Black-Hearted!" Or Serve Up A Cold-Blooded Dose Of Payback!

The Time For Change Had Come. Their Plan Was Now In Effect. They Knew The Danger And Accepted The Challenge. Only 'GOD" Knew What The Result Would Be. And They Were Absolutely Certain "GOD" was On Their Side.

(Continued On Next Page)

The Rally Members Never Imagined An Invasion On Their Own Soil. They Had Disregarded Their Own Security. After All, They Were At Home. Where It's Safe! They Were Family-All For One And One For All! The Self-Proclaimed 'Keepers Of The Gate.' The Architects Of Destiny. Judges And Executioners Of The 'Impure' Souls Of Damnation!

Their Number One Rule Was To Achieve Success, By Any means Necessary. And, The Blood On Their Hands And Forefathers Was A Proud Sentiment Of Their Accomplishments. Generation After Generation, They Had Repeated That History. And They Were Looking Forward To Shaping Young Minds To Accomplish Those Same Goals. And No-One Was Going To Stop Them!

Life Is 90% Mental And 10% Physical. And So, 'As A Man Think It, It Is How It Shall Be.' Just Like Good Soil, Good Thoughts Brings Forth Good Things. Bad Soil Are Things Droughts Are Made Of. The Shadow Of A Man's Character Is In His Mind.

'Samuel Paxton,' The Leader Of 'The Black-Sheep Soldiers' Spoke. "Any Foolish Resistance We'll Start Shooting The Leadership: From The Top Down! Beginning With 'The Grand-Dragon' Himself. You're All Under 'GODS" Arrest! And, HE's Sent Us Here To Deliver The Blow!" As They Disarmed The Real Bandits.

"The Gates Of Hell Are Open! Now, Who Wants To Burn!?" (Silence)... Someone Yelled! "You'll Never Get Out Of Here Alive!" He Was Immediately Met With A Blow To The Head by An AK-47, From One Of The "Black Sheep Soldiers!"

"Speaking Of Death, We Have A Surprise For You." Someone Wheeled In A Cart Full Of Explosives. Enough To Blow The

(Continued On Next Page)

Entire Compound To Smithereens! "A Gift On Your 100th Anniversary From All Of Us! Do The Math, All For One! And One For All!" (Silence.). With Looks Of Horror On The Faces Of The Tied-Up Brotheren, History Was About To Be Made.

Flash Back!

Earlier. Thelma, Billy-Jean And Sister, Along With Some Of Their Girl Friends, Pulled Up In An Open Truck To Deliver (Drugged-Up) Refreshments To The Men Guarding The Gates. Once The Bait Was Taken. The Plan Was In Effect.

"We're Here To Take Care Of Our Men, 'John-Boy'." Spoke Thelma. "I Know My Husband's In There. And, I Just Want To Make Sure He's Well Fed. What's Wrong With That? Besides, We Or Shall I Say, 'Billy-Jean' Brought You Something Too."

"That's Nice Thelma, But You Know Women Aren't Allowed At Our Camps?" Spoke, 'John-Boy'.

'Billy-Jean' Spoke Up In A Sexy Voice. "We Know That Lover-Boy. We Don't Want To Come In. We Know Boys Will Be Boys. Just Like Girls Will Be Girls. We Just Thought You Boys Might Be Hungry?" All Eyes Were On 'Billy-Jean', The Blond Bombshell From Mount Peek.

In The Sweetest Of Voices, 'Billy-Jean' Said, "Do You Want It Or Not?" All The Pretty Smiles Flamed The Moon-Lit Night. As They Opened The Baskets Of Goodies. Everything Looking Delicious, Including the Ladies!

'John-Boy' Spoke Up. "You Know We Do." Smiling A Special Smile For And At 'Billy-Jean'. He And His Buddies Grabbed The Baskets And Crates Of Drinks. All Smiles And In Unison, They Said, "Thanks Ladies'" The Women Smiled As They Drove Out Of Sight.

(Continued On Next Page)

'Sister' Spoke. "I Sure Hope Those "Black Sheep Soldiers" Can Help My Husband Grow Up And Start Living In The 21st Century."

'Thelma' Added, "Well, They Sure Helped My Son. Jeb made A 'Hate-Monger' Out Of Him, From Day One. But, Now he's Doing Missionary Work. Saving Lives And Helping Others. They Did That, And I'm Forever Grateful." All Said, "Amen To That!", As They Drove Back To Town. They Believed The Best Was Yet To Come.

The Present!

The Bombs Were Set To Be Lit. All Tied Up And Ready To Blow, Were The Brotheren. As The Fuse Burned Down, The Dragons Had Horror In Their Eyes. They All Started Wetting And Crapping In Their Pants...

A Fizzle, Then A Popcorn Fart Of An Explosion...All Duds? "What!?" Eyes Of Relief For The Brotheren. You Could Have Filled Up A Truck With All That Manure. "Damn!" That Place Smelled And Resembled A Sewer.

In All The Excitement Nobody Noticed. But A White Envelope Sat On Top Of The Crates Of Explosives. It Read. "Open Me."

So The 'Grand Dragon' Did The Honors And Opened And Read. "Like Prizes In A Cracker-Jack, With Childish Gifts In Paper Sacks. We Just Showed Some Love. Show The World Some Back."

All Smiles And With A Wink! The "Black Sheep-Soldiers" Slipped Off Into The Night. As The Song "The Big-Payback!" By 'James Brown' played in the background.

Excerpt From: "Bad Hair Days!" & "Tales From The Hip!" Collection.

SECTION V

THE Soul-Flow!
(Series)

SPECIAL ADDITION
(12-Episodes)
(6-Herein)

"**Soul-Flow!**" IS AN EXCEPTIONAL HERO DEDICATED TO PROTECTING THE 'HOOD!' HE ONLY COMES OUT AT NIGHT. HIS UNTIRING EFFORTS TO HELP OTHERS IS UNMATCHED AND HE ALWAYS GETS THE JOB DONE.

SO, I INTRODUCE TO YOU THE NEW WAVE OF 'SUPER-HEROES' IN MY 'BAD-HAIR-DAYS!' & 'TALES FROM THE HIP!' COLLECTION...GOD BLESS!

"Soul-Flow!"
'Toxic-Woman The Kiss Of Death!'
(SERIES)

Look!!!...Is It The Word, Is It The Game?

    Yelp! It's 'Soul-Flow!'

    Faster Than A 'Fruit-Fly'.

    More Powerful Than 'Hocus-Pocus!' (Dance)

    Able To Creep Through The Hood Without A Sound.

    (Tip-Toe)

    Can Bend 'Weed' With His Bare-Hands!

.   (A Bent Roll-Up)

    Fighting For Snoops, Busters, Transits And Strays.

Episode: "Toxic-Woman The Kiss Of Death!"

 Word On The Street, 'Toxic-Woman The Kiss Of Death!' It's Up To You "Soul-Flow" To Drop It Like It's Hot!

"What's Up?"...The 'Toxic-Woman's Loose Again, She's Riding The 'Kiss Of Death! Folks Got 'Liquid-Handcuffs' On, Afraid To Move In The 'HOOD'. We Need You To Take The 'Cuffs' Off. So People Can Believe Again."

"She's Popular In The 'HOOD'. She Loves To Beg, Borrow And Steal, Only She Never Pay Back. Now The 'HOOD' Has Put The 'Loan-Freeze' On Her And Put Her On Lock!"

We Had her At The 'Chocolate-Clinic', But She Broke Out Like An Inmate At The 'Afro-Hilton"(Jail-90% Black). Now She Has The "V-Cup-Virus!" We Don't Want Our Folks

With The "Kiss Of Death!" We Need You To Stop It Before It Spreads Like Butter."

"We Got The "All Eyes On Her' Alert. But Nobody's Seen Her...Here's A Bag Of 'Weed' For Your Trouble"...

'Soul-Flow', "This One's On Me!" Off! Off! And Away! Went "Soul-Flow!"

"Soul-Flow' Tip-Toed Through The 'HOOD' Over To 'Flavor-Park', With His 'Fruit-Fly' Speed. 'Soul-Flow' Found Her Sleeping In 'Card-Board-City', The Homeless-Gated Community On The Back End. He Could Hear "Bag-Lady" Playing On The Radio. 'Soul-Flow' Immediately Bent Some "Weed", To Put Everybody On Freeze! Then He Used A 'Germicide-Weed' To Sanitize All Of 'Card-Board-City'. Instantly Killing All Traces Of "The Kiss Of Death!"

Then With His 'Hocus-Pocus' Dance, "Moon-Walked' Over And Put A 'Face-Cup' On 'Toxic-Woman'. She Was Happy To See 'Soul-Flow'. She Knew Who He Was, She Was Happy As 'Butter-Milk-Patty.' All She Wanted Was Help And Some Attention. All-Smiles, Was The 'Toxic-Woman'!

"Soul-Flow', Delivered Her To "Shady's-Hospital", Where They Saved Her Life. And Peace Was Brought Back To The 'HOOD'! Fresh Off The Cuff! Easy-Peezy! The Icing On The Cake. 'Soul-Flow' Had Dropped It Like It's Hot!

(Continued On This Page)

"THANKS, "Soul-Flow!".........."We Can All Believe Again! You've Killed 'The Kiss Of Death!'...All To The Good, "Soul-Flow!"...'Soul-Flow' Gave A Wink and A Nod, And Jetted....Wearing His Pad-Leather Black And Ski-Mask And Took Off Into The Night...So He Could Continue To Give The 'HOOD' Another Taste Of His "Super-Powers!" Again, When He Takes Flight!

Excerpt: From "Bad Hair Days!" & "Tales From The Hip!" Collection.

THE NEW! "Soul-Flow!" SERIES!

"Soul-Flow!"
'Midnight Buffet!'
(SERIES)

Look!!! Is It The Word, Is It The Game?

    Yelp! It's 'Soul-Flow!'

    Faster Than A 'Fruit-Fly'.

    More Powerful Than 'Hocus-Pocus!' (Dance)

    Able To Creep Through The Hood Without A Sound.

    (Tip-Toe)

    Can Bend 'Weed' With His Bare-Hands!

.   (A Bent Roll-Up)

  Fighting For Snoops, Busters, Transits And Strays.

Episode: "Midnight Buffet!"

Word On The Street, 'Midnight Buffet!' Gang Warfare Was In The Air And It Was Up To "Soul-Flow!", To Stop It! "Rev. Good-Heart" From 'Stone-Temple' Baptist Church, Had Set-Up A Meet.

    "What's Up?"..." The Vice-Lords' And 'The Disciples' Are Planning A 'Shot-Out' At Midnight! And We need You To Stop It, And Put Some 'LOVE' Back in the 'HOOD' Again...We All Gotta live!"

    'Rev. Good-Heart' Asked, "What Can I Give You?"

    'Soul-Flow', "This One's On me!" Things Were Getting Out Of Hand In This 'Land Of The Free'. But Stopping 'Beefs' In The 'HOOD', Never Came Easy!

A Lady Who Ran From The 'Boo!' Blood In The 'Sand-Box' Where Bullets Flew. Guns That Blazed And Stuck like Glue!. The Church Had Gotten Beat. Now He Moved A Plan To Stop The 'Blood In The Street...Off! Off! And Away! Went 'Soul-Flow!'

'Soul-Flow', Tip-Toed From Roof-Top To Roof-Top With His 'Fruit-Fly' Speed. And With His '"Hocus-Pocus"', He Danced From Crib To Crib Where The Gang-Members Lived. Bending 'Weed" Like Blindness For A 'Hypnotic-Freeze' On All That Got In His Way!

Bouncing Through Windows Off Every 'Fire-Escape', Now it Was Time To Move On Before It Got Too Late. The 'War-Ground' Was Set For 'Jump-Street' And 'Off-The –Muscle'. Where Kids Played In the Daytime And Players Hustled!

Both Sides Were All 'G'd-Up!, 'Mobbed-Up' And Ready To Go Hard! "Vice-Lords! "Yay!" "Yay!"", And Coming The Other Way. "Disciples! "Yay!" "Yay!"" Who Would Live To See The Dawn Of Another Day?!

They All Saw The Tables All Lined-Up. And Music Was Playing That Made Them Hold-Up. 'Marvin Gaye's, "What's Going On?" Was Playing And Food Was On The Tables. Banners Hung On Both Sides, Clearly Labeled: "Vice-Lords!" And The Other Side, "Disciples!" And In The Middle, A Free-Standing Sign That Read On Both Sides: "The Divide-Neutral-Territory!"

The 'Beef' Was Over Territory And The 'Divide' Happened. As They All Stepped-Up To The Tables. The Food Hitting Their Noses Smelled Sweet! 'Soul-Flow' Was Sitting At The End Of The 'Buffet', With Their Bullets At His Feet.

He Held Up 2-Sacks Of Bullets With Logo's On Them. He Nodded Left It Came Back. He Nodded Right It Came Back, 'The

(Continued On Next Page)

Warrior's Creed Of Honor!' Had "Dapped-Up!" As 'Soul-Flow' Sat On The Sacks Of Stolen-Bullets. The "Nod Of Respect" Was Given To 'Soul-Flow!' For Being A "True-Warrior Of Peace". He Had Disarmed Both Sides Without A Scratch! Then he 'Winked!'

"Rev. Good-Heart" And The "Church-Mothers" Layout Of Fried Chicken, Collard Greens, Mac And Cheese, Peach-Cobbler, Corn-Bread And Sweet-Potato Pie, With A Big 'See-Through' Cooler Full Of Sweet-Tea. It Did What It Was Suppose To Do. To Calm The Brothers Down So Life Could Rule.

Not A Single Shot Was Fired. They Bumped Some 'Weed', Had A Feast, And Remembered The Day When The "HOOD' Had Peace. It Took A Joint Effort But 'Soul-Flow' Had Delivered The Peace, With The "Midnight-Buffet of A Soul-Food Feast!"

"THANKS, 'Soul-Flow!'...You Put Some 'LOVE' Back In The 'HOOD' Again...We All Gotta Live!" After A Long Night, All The Bullets Were Still There The Next Day. "Rev. Good-Heart" Hid Them In The Church. As He Started To 'PRAY', "Soul-Flow, I'll Be Waiting At The Golden-Gates."

'Soul-Flow' Didn't Jet...He Just Walked Away To The Sound Of Music (K C & Jo Jo's "LIFE!"), Of Laughter, And Jokes From The Gangs...Wearing His Pad-Leather Black & Ski-Mask And Stepping Off Into The Night...So He Could Continue to Give The 'HOOD' Another Taste Of His "Super-Powers!" Again, When He Takes Flight!

Excerpt: From "Bad Hair Days!" & "Tales From The Hip!" Collection.

THE NEW! "Soul-Flow!"   SERIES!

"Soul-Flow!"
'BUGGED-OUT!'
(SERIES)

Look!!! Is It The Word, Is It The Game?

      Yelp! It's 'Soul-Flow!'

      Faster Than A 'Fruit-Fly'.

      More Powerful Than 'Hocus-Pocus!' (Dance)

      Able To Creep Through The Hood Without A Sound.

.   (Tip-Toe)

      Can Bend 'Weed' With His Bare-Hands!

.   (A Bent Roll-Up)

  Fighting For Snoops, Busters, Transits And Strays.

Episode: "BUGGED OUT!"

 Word On The Street, 'BUGGED OUT!' "The 'Trailer-Park' Roaches Are Taking Over The 'HOOD'. We Want It Stopped!...They're Not Our Roaches 'Get'em-Up-Outta' Here! That's What's Up!"

    "...They're All Over The Projects. Invading our Happy Homes. We Tried Stomping, Smoking And Choking Them Out! But They Still Live! No Matter What We Do To Them, They Won't Give!"

    "...We Just Want To Live In Harmony. Here's A Bag Of "Weed" For Your Trouble Yay!"...Off! Off! And Away! Went "Soul-Flow!"

(Continues On This Page)

Soul-Flow, 'Tip-Toed' Over To The Projects With His 'Fruit-Fly' Speed. There Were 2-Kinds Of Roaches-American-Made, Friendly, Ready To Die, And Easy To Kill. But Those 'German-Trailer-Park' Roaches Had Steel Backs, Armor-All-Senses. Immune To Toxics And Drank 'Bug-Killer' Like Ice-Water. A Serious Foe In The 'HOOD'. Who Couldn't Be Slaughtered.

'Soul-Flow', Used His 'Hocus-Pocus' As He Danced Through The Streets. Then He Turned Up The Music To An 'Old-School' Beat. "Another One Bites The Dust!" The German-Marching Song.

They Filed Out One By One Humming Along. Then, 'Soul-Flow' Bent Some 'Special-Weed,'-Fake-Crystal-That The German-Roaches Love. They All Came Out Of Hiding Marching Down The Street. Following 'Soul-Flow' And Stepping To The Beat. Just Like German Soldiers On 'Doomsday'.

The 'HOOD' Just Loved Watching Their Parade. Like That Perfect Soldier All Lined Up! For A Late Night Stroll. A 'Super-Fly' Moment To Reflect The 'HOOD' had had Enough!

"Soul-Flow", Dropped Off Those Roaches At The 'Ball N Chain' Trailer-Park. But They Already Had Roaches.

(Continues On Next Page)

This Created A Spark! There Was No Coming Back To The 'HOOD'. The 'HOOD' had Locked Them Out! Now The World Was Made For Living. Now What's That All About?

The Roaches Lined Up From Both Sides. For A 'Battle-Royale' That Would Be Fought With Pride. The 'Trailer-Park' Roaches Were Wearing "MAGA" Hats. While The 'Hooded-Out!' Roaches Wore Bandanas And 'Doo-Rags', Were Ready To Fight And Started To Brag. Like A 'Mexican-Stand-Off' They Gave A Visual And Realized That They Were Related 4-Show!(Sure).

It Was All Good In The 'HOOD', They Came To Find Out That They Were Cousins. From The Song & Dance, They Started 'Buggin!' They All Dropped Their Weapons And Hugged-Up! A Great Day In The 'Ball N Chain' Trailer-Park For A Grand Hook-Up!. They Celebrated Their Unity In Their Community!

"THANKS 'Soul-Flow!'... As He Fell Back Into The 'HOOD'..."We Can All Live In Harmony Again!" Both sides were Happy, The 'HOOD' Lived Again. The 'German Roaches Had Found More Than Their Brothers. But Their Long-Lost Twins! You might Lock-Out A Brother, But Let The Twins In.

(Continues On Next Page)

"Soul-Flow" Jetted!...Wearing His Pad-Leather Black & Ski-Mask And Took Off Into The Night...So He Could Continue to Give The 'HOOD' Another Taste Of His "Super-Powers!" Again, When He Takes Flight!

Excerpt: From "Bad Hair Days!" & "Tales From The Hip!" Collection.

THE NEW! "Soul-Flow!" SERIES!

"Soul-Flow!"

'Help, Amigo! Save The Babies!'
(SERIES)

Look!!! Is It The Word, Is It The Game?

    Yelp! It's 'Soul-Flow!'

    Faster Than A 'Fruit-Fly'.

    More Powerful Than 'Hocus-Pocus!' (Dance)

    Able To Creep Through The Hood Without A Sound...

.   (Tip-Toe)

    Can Bend 'Weed' With His Bare-Hands!

.   (A Bent Roll-Up)

  Fighting For Snoops, Busters, Transits And Strays.

Episode: "Help Amigo! Save The Babies!"

Word On The Street, 'Help Amigo! Save The Babies!' It's Up To You My Amigo, "SOUL-FLOW!," To Bring Back Our Babies.

    "What's Up?"... The Government Has Taken Them On The Other Side Of The Border. And We Want Them Home Amigo. Family Is Everything To Us. We Will Be Forever In Your Debt, 'Soul-Flow!'

    "...I Have Some Of The Best 'Mexican-Bud' For Your Troubles...Please Help 'Save The Babies.' Our 'Bam-Binos': 'Santino, Tortino And Harpo, Have Their 'Cousins': Holio, Colio And Boolio With Them. "Sietta, Regretta And Zeta", Are Our Girls And They Miss Their Brothers. And 'Mami' Won't Stop Crying To 'Papi'...We All Just Want To Live!"

(Continues On This Page)

'Soul-Flow', "This One's On Me!" Off! Off! And Away! Went 'Soul-Flow!'

'Soul-Flow' Tip-Toed Over To The Other Side Of Town With His 'Fruit-Fly' Speed. Once At The Airport, 'Soul-Flow' Capped-Out His Black-Poncho. And With His 'Hocus-Pocus', He Catapulted And Jet-Leaped! Over The Security Fence And Started 'Moon-Walking' With A Spice Of 'Cha, Cha, Cha, Across The Air-Field.

'Soul-Flow' Bent Some "Weed", Which Hypnotized Security And Froze Them In Their Tracks! With An Extra Dose Of His 'Fruit-Fly' Speed And 'Hocus-Pocus', 'Soul-Flow' Painted And Erased The "B" And Turned The "L" Into A "P" On The 'Good-Year-Blimp'. That Now Read. "The Good-Year-Pimp". He Jacked And Borrowed It For The Journey On The Other Side Of The Boarder.

'Soul-Flow' Knew The 'Pimp-Blimp' Could Not Be Detected By Radar. Since It Was Not Metal Radio-Waves Could Not Flag, The 'Hooded-Out" Air-Bag.

'Soul-Flow' Landed In 'Taco-Ville' Next To 'Burrito-Village'. Where Family On The Other-Side, Had been Tapped To Be At the Ready! 'Holio, Colio And Boolio' Were The 1st On Board. Followed By 'Santino, Tortino And Harpo, Followed By Their 'Cousin', "Hoop-Po". Who Was Ready For A New Life In The "HOOD'.

(Continues On Next Page)

All In All, Between The Little 'Senoritas' And 'Bam-Binos'...'Soul-Flow' Counted 25 Little-Ones. It Was A Smooth Ride Home. After The Long-Good-Byes (Hasta la vista), And Strong-Hello's (Mucho-Ola's), They Landed In The Heart Of The 'HOOD' Under The cover Of Night, To A Song Called, 'The Burrito-Bandito!'...

" I Yi YiYi, I Am The Burrito-Bandito! You Give Me Tacos And I'll Be Your Friend. The Burrito-Bandito! Until The End!...I Yi YiYi, I Am The Burrito-Bandito!" And So It Sung...As 'Soul-Flow' Put A Little Cha, Cha, Cha! On It! With His 'Hocus-Pocus' Moves!

They Prepared A 'Mexican-Feast', A 'Fiesta For The Siesta!'...A 'Pinata' For The Kids, And 'Tequila' (Mexican-Vodka), For The 'Grown-Folks'. It Never Felt So Good In The 'HOOD!' With A Brown & Black Block-Party!

...Even The 'Stripper-Mamas' From "Hot-Cakes" And "Spanish-Harlem", Made Their Favorite Dish. But They Ate It Anyway. Back Together Again.

"THANKS "Soul-Flow!"...We Can All Live Again! You're Our Hero! Amigo!"...'Soul-Flow' Didn't Jett. He Just Eased Into The Night...And So They Sang!... "Havana Um La

(Continues On Next Page)

La, In Savannah Our 'Hacienda' Ha Ha Ha"...Wearing His Pad-Leather Black & Ski-Mask...So He Could Continue To Give The 'HOOD' Another Taste Of His 'Super-Powers!' Again, When He Takes Flights!

Excerpt: From "Bad Hair Days!" & "Tales From The Hip!" Collection.

THE NEW! "Soul-Flow!" SERIES!

"SOUL-FLOW!"
'Po Po Brutality!'
(SERIES)

Look!!! Is It The Word, Is It The Game?

     Yelp! It's 'Soul-Flow!'

     Faster Than A 'Fruit-Fly'.

     More Powerful Than 'Hocus-Pocus!' (Dance)

     Able To Creep Through The Hood Without A Sound.

     (Tip-Toe)

     Can Bend 'Weed' With His Bare-Hands!

.   (A Bent Roll-Up)

  Fighting For Snoops, Busters, Transits And Strays.

Episode: "Po Po Brutality!"

Word On The Street,...'Po Po Brutality!' We Need To Calm These Fools!...

  "What's Up?"... "5-OH! Been Off The Chain With All These Dropped-Bodies Of Young Minorities And Getting A Pass From Their Majority. We Need You To Flavor The Line...We All Gotta Live! What's The Price?"

  'Soul-Flow', This One's On Me!...Off! Off! And Away! Went 'Soul-Flow!'

  "Soul-Flow" Tip-Toed Over To A Pay-Phone, In The Heart Of The 'HOOD', With His 'Fruit-Fly' Speed. He Dropped A 'Fake-Call', To Set 'Po PO' Up! That A 'White-Woman' Was Thrown Under The Bus, At The Corner Of 'Sport' And 'Crime'.

Putting On The Jets In 60 Seconds or Less, As Soon As 'PO Po' Jumped From Behind The Wheel. 'Soul-Flow', Pushed Them Back On Their Heels.

'Soul-Flow', With His 'Hocus-Pocus' Danced Through The Street And 'Jacked!', 'Po Po's Whip! Like A Real Hero! He Had Called The Crew To Soften The Blow. The Best Chop-Shop In The 'HOOD'!

Run By 'Leroy, Tyrone And Salam', With 'Carlos, Marlos And Big-Barlos'-The Man!, On 'Tops & Bottoms'. It Was All For The Token, Unspoken. These Men Don't Phase, They Got 'Big-Boy' Ways! When 'Soul-Flow' Spoke On The List, With Just Head-Nods, They 'Tricked-Out!' Po Po's Wheels And Gave It A Twist.

With No Way To Call For Back-Up. 'Po Po' Walked The 'HOOD' For Hours. Like Unarmed Bandits That Lost Their Powers. But, Before The 'Po Po' Could Get All "Fluffed!" The 'Po Po' Mobile Just Popped Up! With Dice Hanging From The Rear-View.

'Soul-Flow' Stood Nearby With A Sign At His Feet. That Said, "A Gift From The 'HOOD' Now Leave Us Be!"...'Soul-Flow' Bent Some "Weed" To Calm These Fools. And Made Them Appreciate The New! 'Po Po Whip' (Shining Like A New Penny!), And Forget About That Moment's Interlude.

The 'Po Po Whip' That Had Just Got 'Jacked' Was All' Tricked-Out! With A TV-Antenna In The Back. It Had A 'Gangsta-Sound-System' That Played, "Diggin In The Scene With A Gangsta Lean." Sporting Gangsta-White-Wall Tires, With A 'Candy-Apple-Red' Paint Job.

The "Weed" Mixed With The Music Had Them 'Bobble-Headed' And 'Thumpin', And His White-Partner Even Started 'Fist-Pumpin', As Onlookers Watched And Smiled.

Upon Closer Observation, It Had A Combo-Automatic-Donut-Maker And Oven, In The Backseat. Flagging A Milk-Shake-Fountain In The Front, With A Mini-Bar Sitting At The Knee!

"Po Po' Realized That When It Came To All Things, America Was Still On Top. Then They Noticed The Sticker On The Dash That Read, "Po Po Brutality Is A Condition Of The Heart." The 'Weed' That 'Soul-Flow' Had Bent, Made Them See Reality, To Serve And Protect the Whole Community.

'Po Po' Sat On Plush Seats With Nothing But Smiles, As They Rode In Style Riding Those Brakes. Waving At All Residents, While Eating Donuts And Drinking Milk-Shakes. 'Soul-Flow' Stood On A Hill With 'The Crew', As They Nodded In Unison. Something All Good In The 'HOOD' Was About To Begin. 'Po Po' Showed Nothing But 'Love' Every Day. In The 'Tricked-Out' Ride, And A 'Ghetto-Buffet'. The Truth Of The Matter Is Not All Cops Are 'BAD". It's Just That "Dirty-Few", Who's Bent On Making Life Sad!

(Continues On this Page)

"THANKS, "Soul-Flow!".........."We Can All Live Again!" As He
Jetted, They All "Dapped' While Wearing A Grin....Wearing His
Pad-Leather Black And Ski-Mask And Took Off Into The
Night...So He Could Continue To Give The 'HOOD' Another Taste
Of His "Super-Powers!" Again, When He Takes Flight!

..."Extra! Extra! Read All About It!"
'The Powers That Be'... Offered Point-Blank 'Soul-Flow' An
Award, But He Said, "No Thanks. I'll Only Give It Back!...Just
Keep Doing What You're Doing, There's No Need for That."

Excerpt: From "Bad Hair Days!" & "Tales From The Hip!"
Collection.

THE NEW! "Soul-Flow!" SERIES!

"Soul-Flow!"
'Basket-Case!'
(SERIES)

Look!!! Is It The Word, Is It The Game?

       Yelp! It's 'Soul-Flow!'

       Faster Than A 'Fruit-Fly'.

       More Powerful Than 'Hocus-Pocus!' (Dance)

       Able To Creep Through The Hood Without A Sound.

       (Tip-Toe)

       Can Bend 'Weed' With His Bare-Hands!

.   (A Bent Roll-Up)

  Fighting For Snoops, Busters, Transits And Strays.

Episode: "Basket-Case!"

Word On The Street, 'Basket-Case!' "Daddy's In Jail And Mama's On The Street, These Kids Won't Make It Without Nothing To Eat." Spoke, 'BJ', Holding A Basket And Sippin 'Kool-Aid'. With A Sucker's-Parched Face And Hair All Laid.

   "What's Shaken?"... "Need To Find A Home For The Twins; 'Frick & Frat', For a Better Chance Across The Track. These Twins Have No Back, Their Spines Are Weak As Water. In This 'HOOD' Of Ours, They'll Only Get Slaughtered! 'Twins In A Basket', Beats How We found Them, Lying In A Casket."

(Continues On Next Page)

"They Need A Chance To 'Man-Up!' And Be Tough!
Their 'Mommy & Poppy' Didn't Love Them Enough...So
Here's A Bag Of 'Weed' For Your Troubles Yay!"

'Soul-Flow', Pushed Back The 'Weed' To "BJ" And Took The
Basket And Nodded Out...Off! Off! And Away! Went 'Soul-Flow!'

"Soul-Flow" Tip-Toed Through The "HOOD' To The Top Of
The Hill, "Suburbie-Heaven", 'Big-Dollars' Were Real. Real-
Dollars Stacked High And Deep. Never A Problem Every Day Of
The Week. As He Crossed The Line With His 'Fruit-Fly' Speed.
He thought About "Apple-Jack", A Brother In Need.

'Apple-Jack' Cleaned It Up! An 'All-Out Stunner', Who Once
Lived in The 'Bluff!' Put On The "HOOD's "No-Sell-List",
Because Drugs Brought Him Down And Had Given Him Fits! So
The 'Dealer's Creed' Was He Can't Buy This.

'Apple-Jacks' "HOOD-NAME' Use To Be "Filthy-McNasty!" A
'HOOD-RAT' Turned Square, Was Now The Owner Of A 'Car-
Wash-Dynasty!' 'Soul-Flow' Cleaned Him Up!, And Led Him Out
Of The 'Bluff!'And Created The 'Drug-Dealer's Creed' That Put
Him On 'Cuffs'.

He Lived On The Hill With "Last-Chance-Melinda", After
They Hooked-Up! 'Melinda' Couldn't Have Kids, So They Didn't
Have Any. "Xmas." Was Coming And Their Wish Was Not For
Just One, But To Have Many.

"Soul-Flow" ,Knocked On The Door With Basket In Hand.
With No Doubt In His Mind, That This Is Where, The Twins
Would Land.

(Continues On Next Page)

Both, 'Melinda & Apple-Jack' Were Wearing A Grin. 'Apple-Jack' Instantly Recognized His Long-Time-Friend.
No Questions Asked, Just Tears Of Joy. When 'Melinda' Saw That Basket Of Those Handsome Boys.

'Apple-Jack' Still kept His Ear To The Street. He Knew 'Soul-Flow' Was More than A 'Street-Soldier', Who Protected The Weak. The Brother's Bonded, No Need To Bend 'Weed'. 'Melinda' Never looked Happier With Those Twins On Her Knees.

A Beautiful Christmas-Tree And The house All Lit. No Need For 'Hocus-Pocus' It was All Legit. Offerings Of Blessings To A Long-Time-Friend. It's Always Where You're Going Not Where You've Been.

"THANKS, "Soul-Flow!".........""We're Family Again!" And Most Of All Thank You for Being A Friend... Hell, 'Soul-Flow' Almost Spent The Night, But A lot Of 'Xmas.' To Be Had Was Needed In The 'HOOD'. For The Less Fortunate And Misunderstood... Like 'Santa-Claus', 'Soul-Flow' Had Just Set-It-Off!...Dropping Twins To A Couple, After They Made Boss!...Their 'Xmas-Wish' Had Been Fulfilled, on A Family They Could Build. To A Family That Came From The 'HOOD' And Now Lived On The Hill... So He Jetted... Wearing

(Continues On Next Page)

His Pad-Leather Black And Ski-Mask And Took Off Into The Night...So He Could Continue To Give The 'HOOD' Another Taste Of His "Super-Powers!" Again, When He Takes Flight!

Excerpt: From "Bad Hair Days!" & "Tales From The Hip!" Collection.

THE NEW! "Soul-Flow!" SERIES!

BONUS SECTIONS:

CHARACTER LISTINGS
THE LYRICAL MASTER (List of Songs-Available)
COMMENTARY & SUMMARY

CHARACTER LISTINGS

List of Characters
(The King Of Clean)

The Laundry Wizard

List Of Characters
(Cats, Rats & Candles)

Lucky The Burglar   Mrs. Weedermire
Miles (The Cat)

List of Characters
(Sweet Air Lane)

Stucky	Lady-Z
Aunt Bella	Big-Bertha
Fragile-Rock (Slim-Goody)	Betty-Boo
Brenda-Boo	Lady-Sue
Buddy-B	Bubbles

List of Characters
(Bonnie & Pride)

Bonnie	Pride
Bobby Upshaw	

List Of Characters
(Midnight Swim)

Willie The Wino	Harry The Hippie
Ms. Chestnut	The Dogs
Po Po	

List Of Characters
(You Ain't White Enough)

The Grand Dragon

Billy-Jean

Thelma

Jeb

The Black Sheep Soldiers

Samuel Paxton

Sister

John-Boy

The Brotheren (The Dragons)

List Of Characters
(Soul-Flow!-Series)

Soul-Flow!

Sugar-Baby

German-Roaches

German-Trailer-Park-Roaches

Tortino

Holio

Boolio

Regretta

Mami

Hoop-Po

Bam-Binos

Po Po

Leroy

Salam

Marlos

BJ

Last-Chance-Melinda

Mommy

Toxic-Woman

Ms. Get-Right!

American-Roaches

Santino

Harpo

Colio

Sietta

Zeta

Papi

Senoritas

Stripper-Mamas

White-Woman

Tyrone

Carlos

Big-Barlos

Apple-Jack (Filthy-McNasty)

Frick & Frat

Poppy

THE LYRICAL MASTER
(List of Songs Available)

Listings Under Musical Categories:

ROCK & ROLL

1. King of The Band
2. The Tattoo Blues & Piercing Pains
3. Fluffy
4. Bad Girls
5. Wrinkles In My Mind
6. Snowball's chance In Hell!
7. The One-Eyed devil
8. Lady-Friend
9. Stick To Your Guns
10. Super-Villain
11. The Magic Wand

REGGAE

1. Beauty Til it's Skin Deep
2. Coco Love
3. Sand In My Snowflakes
4. A Quarter To Get up!
5. My Own Plan
6. Just Call Me Satan
7. No Soup For You
8. The Shante
9. Have I got A Song For You
10. Monkey In My Pants
11. Secret Indictment
12. Trouser Monkey

COUNTRY & WESTERN

1. On All Sides
2. Midnight Train
3. Ain't No Fun
4. I Want My Job Back!

JAZZ

1. Ciara
2. Brain Food

GOSPEL

1. All To The Good
2. Sacrificial Lamb
3. A Soldier In GOD'S Army
4. Hearts' Communicate
5. When Doves Fly
6. Heaven's In Store
7. Blessed & Highly Favored!
8. The Lord Wants U-2-Rule
9. Help Somebody
10. We Thank You

RHYTHM & BLUES

1. The Rhythm Of My Soul
2. Can't Sleep
3. The Right Dream
4. What Makes You Better?
5. Loves Track
6. Bullet-Proof Fantasy!
7. Our Dirty Laundry
8. Stone Romance
9. Hearts Communicated
10. Sugar Melts
11. Chocolate Covered (C-Apples)
12. Lost Love Never Ends

THE LYRICAL MASTER
(Songs Continue)

GOSPEL

11. The Ages
12. The Invisible Sword
13. A Miracle For You!
14. Lord I'm Home
15. Show Me Where GOD'S At?
16. Touching lives
17. Let Your Light Shine
18. Liberate All-The-Saints
19. All Around Me
20. Book of Remembrance

POP & HIP-HOP

1. Do The Math
2. Someone Like That?
3. Busy-Body!
(Keep That Body Busy!)
4. The-Na-Way-Yay!
5. Beat Around The Bush
6. Bodacious!
7. Let's Talk About
Something Else
8. In The Way
9. The Boo! Game
10. Games People Play
11. His-Story Not Mine!
12. Mr. Freeze
13. Recognize

COMMERCIAL (JINGLES)
1. Put a Spin On It!
2. No! More! Commercials!
2. A Treasure-Chest Full of Goodies
3. More Bang For The Buck!

VARIETY
(Unique & Different)

1. Victoria's Got A Secret
2. Scooby Popped A Square
3. Come Get Your Medicine
4. Jealousy Rained On Me

RAP & R & B (Mixed)

14. Dynamite Hill
15. Dry-Snitching
16. Ghetto-Butt
17. Tobias
18. The Needy Not The Greedy!

RAP & R & B (Mixed)

1.Rough & Tumble
2. Get In The Game
3. Done Came Up!
4. Y U Wanna Give Up!
5. The Real Police
6. The Dirty-Work
7. Blood On His Hands
. Victory Hill
9. Enough Said
10. You See Too Much!
11. Top Out!
12. Thuggie-Bear
13. Froze Out!

THE LYRICAL MASTER
NEW SONG LIST 2020

GOSPEL

1. All To The Good!
2. Show Me Where "GOD's" AT?
3. Proud Out Loud!

POP & HIP-HOP

1. Pay Me!
2. Beat Around The Bush!
3. Someone Like That!

REGGAE

1. My Own Plan
2. Coconut Rum!

RAP & R & B (Mixed)

1. All In!
2. Treat Me Good

RHYTHM & BLUES

1.Castles In The Sand
2. Curtains Of Love

THE LYRICAL MASTER
(SONGS END!)

COMMENTARY-SUMMARY

THIS BOOK WAS WRITTEN WITH SOMETHING FOR EVERYONE; PEOPLE OF ALL AGES, COLORS AND NATIONALITIES. MY INTENTION IS TO OPEN YOUR MIND TO THE WORLD OF THINKING. IT'S ONE OF MY CONTRIBUTIONS TO HUMANITY.

ALL CREDIT SHOULD BE GIVEN TO GOD; NOT ME OR THOSE WHO INFLUENCED THESE WORKS. OUR ONLY WISH IS FOR PEOPLE TO LEARN TO BE MORE CREATIVE, AND TO LET LOVE IN.

THIS BOOK IS A CONDENSED VERSION OF MY THREE BOOKS. PLUS THE NEW ENTRIES RECENTLY CREATED. THESE EXCERPTS ARE AMONGST THE BEST OF THE PREVIOUS AND THE NEW:

1. TOBIAS'S BOOK OF LYRICAL SONGS
2. TOBIAS'S BOOK OF SONGS AND POEMS
3. TOBIAS'S BOOK OF POEMS, SONGS AND SHORT-

STORIES
(SHORT-STORIES FROM MY NEW! SERIES; "BAD HAIR DAYS" AND "TALES FROM THE HIP!").

THE INFAMOUS HOUSEHOLD READS COLLECTION-WILL MAKE GREAT HOME-POSTERS.

1.THE MIND'S EYE DEFINED!---LONDON 2010, THIS BOOK WAS INTENDED TO OPEN YOUR MIND'S EYE.
2. HAT'S OFF!---A TRIBUTE TO WOMEN IN AN IMPERFECT WORLD; WRITTEN JAN 28TH 2020.
3. THE HONEY CONE HIGHWAY!---WRITTEN FEB 16TH 2020.
4. ALL IN!---WRITTEN MARCH 18TH 2020, GHOST-WRITER...POWER OF THE PEN!.

5. THE WORLD ON PAUSE!---WRITTEN MARCH 23RD 2020, GOD'S WORLD PUT ON PAUSE.

6. AN APPRECIATION OF LIFE!---WRITTEN NOV 23RD 2019, DEDICATED TO MY SON & NEPHEW!

7. STOLEN SUNDAY!---WRITTEN NOV 17TH 2019, BLESSED AND HIGHLY FAVORED.

8. PROUD OUT LOUD!---WRITTEN NOV 11TH 2019, DEDICATED TO DACUMOS & CHRISTELLE'S WEDDING...SONG & POEM. (PHILIPINES).

9. IN A CLASS BY YOURSELF---WRITTEN MARCH 4TH 2020, CONTINUE TO BE A BLESSING TO OTHERS.

10. A LOVE CASTLE---WRITTEN NOV 15TH 2019, WHAT A LOVE PALACE SHOULD BE.

11. SELF SERVING LIES!---WRITTEN FEB 4TH 2020, THE NEW WORLD OF LIES & SECRETS.

12. NOT USE TO MONEY---WRITTEN FEB 19TH 2020, FOR THE GOLD DIGGER IN YOU! MONEY-FOOLS.

13. WHITE DEATH!---WRITTEN DEC 31ST 2001, JUST SAY NO! DRUGS DON'T CARE WHO USE THEM.

POETRY IN MOTION (SECTION II)

1.THE MIND'S EYE SHATTERED!---WRITTEN MARCH 7TH 2020, READERS OF MY 1ST BOOK YOU'RE THE REASON FOR THE 2ND MIND'S EYE SHATTERED! ALSO DEDICATED TO MY BROTHER, 'SIR CHARLES'.

2. LIVING LIFE IN A BOX---WRITTEN OCT 24TH 2019, ENCOURAGEMENT FOR THOSE FROZEN IN TIME.

3. DIGITAL TEMPER TANTRUM!---WRITTEN MARCH 2ND 2020, HANDLE BEEF WITH TACT & CLASS.

4. FIGHTING YOURSELF!---WRITTEN NOV 10TH 2019, FIGHTING YOURESLF TO BE YOURSELF.

5. GLAZED DONUTS!---WRITTEN FEB 2ND 2020, THIRST TRAPPIN...'ALL ABOUT ME DISEASE'.

6. TUGGING AT MY HEART---WRITTEN FEB 20TH 2020, CURTAINS OF LOVE! (SONG & POEM).

7. HELP DON'T CARE!---WRITTEN MARCH 16TH 2020, SPEAKING FOR THE LESS FORTUNATE! DELIVER THE LOVE!

8. LOVE'S PRISON!---WRITTEN MARCH 8TH 2020, DISTANCE LOVERS...TO MY DOVES "TOM & GERI".

9. THE LONG HANDLED SPOON---WRITTEN JAN 13TH 2020, HATERS AND JEALOUSY KEPT AT BAY.

10. PUBLIC LOVE---WRITTEN MARCH 15TH 2020, REAL LOVE PUT TO THE TEST.

11. EARLY BIRD SPECIAL!---WRITTEN SEPT 10TH 2018, EXTRA EFFORT REWARDED.

12. JUST NEXT THEM!---WRITTEN NOV 13TH 2019, SCAMMERS BEWARE!

13. TREAT ME GOOD---WRITTEN FEB 28TH 2020, FOR THE LOVER IN YOU!

14. PUPPIES & WOLVES!---WRITTEN JAN 24TH 2020, MY NEW CHARACTER "FANGS!"...AN ANIMAL HERO STORY.

15. LIFE'S LESSONS---WRITTEN OCT 24TH 2019, DEDICATED TO MY SON.

16. RAPING MEN'S POCKETS!---WRITTEN JAN 30TH 2020, GUIDANCE.

17. NEW YEARS RESOLUTION!---WRITTEN DEC 31ST 2019, A REASON FOR THE SEASON.

18. THE LONE WARRIOR!---WRITTEN MARCH 9TH 2020, BATTLE TESTED!

19. DRUG DEALERS BEWARE!---WRITTEN JAN 29TH 2020, JUST DUE!

20. THE TATTO BLUES!---WRITTEN FEB 2005, POEM & SONG. SIGNED SEALED AND DELIVERED.

21. GOOD N A BAD WAY!---WRITTEN SEPT 29TH 2019, THE GOOD BAD AND THE UGLY.

POETIC-JINGLES & SONGS-WITH OVER 100 SONGS AVAILABLE TO THE ARTISTS IN EVERY MUSICAL CATEGORY; GOSPEL, ROCK

& ROLL, COUNTRY, SOUL, R&B, RAGGAE, AND COMBINATION SONGS (RAP).

1.	CASTLES IN THE SAND===MARCH 14TH 2020
2.	CURTAINS OF LOVE===FEB 20TH 2020
3.	ALL TO THE GOOD!===DEC 28TH 2001
4.	SOMEONE LIKE THAT!===MARCH 24TH 2005
5.	COCONUT RUM!===JAN 13TH 2019
6.	SHOW ME WHERE GOD'S AT?===MAY 2010
7.	ALL IN!===MARCH 18TH 2020
8.	MY OWN PLAN===MARCH 29TH 2005
9.	TREAT ME GOOD===MARCH 14TH 2020
10.	PROUD OUT LOUD!===NOV 11TH 2019
11.	BEAT AROUND THE BUSH!===JAN 1ST 2002
12.	PAY ME!===FEB 17TH 2020

POETIC-STORIES- 'LET'S STOP PLAYING THE VIOLIN AND START PLAYING THE TRUMPET.' IN OTHER WORDS, LET'S NOT HARP ON THE BAD...JUST FIX OUR PROBLEMS AND MOVE FORWARD. THE AUTHOR HAS 17 ADDITIONAL POETIC-SHORT-STORIES FORTHCOMING.

1.	THE KING OF CLEAN!===FEB 23RD 2020
2.	CATS, RATS & CANDLES===JAN 1ST 2002
3.	SWEET AIR LANE!===JAN 11TH 2002
4.	BONNIE & PRIDE!===MARCH 22ND 2009
5.	MIDNIGHT SWIM===JAN 9TH 2002
6.	YOU AIN'T WHITE ENOUGH!===2006

POETIC-STORIES
THE Soul-Flow! (SERIES)
"SPECIAL ADDITION"
(Section V)

1.TOXIC-WOMAN THE KISS OF DEATH!===MARCH 21ST 2020

2. HOT-CAKES!===FEB 29TH 2020

3. BUGGED-OUT!===JAN 13TH 2020

4. HELP AMIGO! SAVE THE BABIES===MARCH 11TH 20205.

5. PO PO BRUTALITY!===FEB 29TH 2020

6. BASKET CASE!===FEB 27TH 2020

BONUS SECTION:

CHARACTER LISTINGS---CHIEF CHARACTERS ALONG WITH ADDITONAL CHARACTERS LISTED FROM THE EXTENDED/BOOK VERSION OF THESE SHORT-STORIES.

www.ingramcontent.com/pod-product-compliance
Lightning Source LLC
Chambersburg PA
CBHW070209200626
46809CB00019B/1717